Timothy and Titus

Baker Bible Guides

General Editors:
Ian Coffey and Stephen Gaukroger

Old Testament Editor: Stephen Dray
New Testament Editor: Stephen Motyer

Isaiah: Philip Hacking
Mark: David Hewitt
Acts: Stephen Gaukroger
1 Corinthians: Robin Dowling
    and Stephen Dray
Ephesians: Stephen Motyer
Philippians: Ian Coffey
1 Peter: Andrew Whitman

Timothy and Titus

Michael Griffiths

Baker Books
A Division of Baker Book House Co.
Grand Rapids, Michigan 49516

Published by Baker Books
a division of Baker Book House Company
P.O. Box 6287, Grand Rapids, MI 49516-6287

First American edition, 1996

Printed in the United States of America

First published in 1996 by Crossway Books
Leicester, England

Library of Congress Cataloging-in-Publication Data

Griffiths, Michael, 1928–
    Timothy and Titus / Michael Griffiths.
      p. cm. — (Baker Bible guides)
    Includes bibliographical references.
    ISBN 0-8010-5733-7 (pbk.)
    1. Bible. N.T. Pastoral Epistles—Commentaries. I. Title.
II. Series.
BS2735.3.G75 1996
227'.8307—dc20   96-46092

For information about academic books, resources for Christian leaders, and all new releases available from Baker Book House, visit our web site:
http://www.bakerbooks.com

Contents

Welcome! 9
How to use your Baker Bible Guide 10
Finding your way round this book 17
Chronology of St Paul's life 19
Map of Asia Minor 21
Introducing Paul's letters to Timothy and
   Titus 22

Paul's greetings to Timothy 1:1–2 23

1 Warning against False Teachers *1 Tim.* 29
Beware false teaching! 1:3b–7
The purpose of the law 1:8–11
How God revolutionized Paul's life 1:12–17
Back to the problem of false teaching 1:18–20

2 Current Errors Explored *1 Tim.* 45
Prayer should be offered for everyone 2:1–7
Men and women at worship 2:8–10
Muzzle the female false teachers! 2:11–12
Three errors of the false teachers 2:13–15

3 Finding New Church Leaders *1 Tim.* 71
Qualities to be looked for in overseers 3:1–7
Qualities to be looked for in deacons 3:8–13
Paul's reason for writing 3:14–16

4 False Teaching Refuted *1 Tim.* 85
False teaching refuted by sound teaching 4:1–5
The marks of a true teacher 4:6–16

Contents

5 Caring for People   *1 Tim.*   **97**
  Caring for widows   5:1–10
  Merry widows   5:6, 11–16
  Elders good and bad   5:17–25

6 Coping with Market Forces   *1 Tim.*   **109**
  Some words for the under class   6:1–2
  Religious people who love money   6:3–10
  Paul's personal charge to Timothy   6:11–16
  Advice to those who are already rich   6:17–21

7 A Task for Titus in Crete   *Titus*   **125**
  Introduction to Titus
  Opening greeting   1:1–4
  The new eldership   1:5–9
  Dealing with false teachers   1:10–16

8 Blameless Living   *Titus*   **141**
  A teaching programme for young and old   2:1–8
  Christians who are slaves   2:9–10
  Christ's beauty and the beastly Cretans   2:11–15

9 Practical Good Works   *Titus*   **153**
  How to achieve a radical change in
    lifestyle   3:1–8a
  Parting instructions   3:8b–15

10 Don't Be Ashamed   *2 Tim.*   **163**
  Introduction to 2 Timothy
  Greetings from death row   1:1–5
  Fan into flame the Spirit's gifts   1:6–7
  Timothy is not to be ashamed   1:8–11
  Paul is not ashamed   1:12–14
  Onesiphorus is not ashamed   1:15–18

11 Working in God's Strength   *2 Tim.*   **177**
  Teaching gifts are to be shared   2:1–2

Understanding hardship   2:3–7
Paul's example of sufferings   2:8–13
Be sensitive to Scripture   2:14–19
Be sensitive to sin and to people   2:20–26

12 The Power of the Scriptures   *2 Tim.*   **195**
A cry from the heart   3:1–4:8
Outwardly godly but powerless   3:1–9
Following Paul's example   3:10–13
The value of Scripture   3:14–17

13 Paul's Last Words   *2 Tim.*   **207**
A solemn charge   4:1–4
Fight the good fight   4:5–8
Some personal messages   4:9–13
Paul leans on the Lord   4:14–18
Final greetings   4:19–22

For Further Reading   223

Welcome!

These days, meeting together to study the Bible appears to be a booming leisure-time activity in many parts of the world. These Bible guides have been designed to help such groups and, in particular, those who lead them, but they are also eminently suitable for individual study.

We are also aware of the needs of those who preach and teach to larger groups as well as the hard-pressed student, all of whom often look for a commentary that gives a concise summary and lively application of a particular passage.

We have therefore enlisted authors who are in the business of teaching the Bible to others and are doing it well. They have kept in their sights two clear aims:

1. To explain and apply the message of the Bible in non-technical language.
2. To encourage discussion, prayer and action on what the Bible teaches.

All of us engaged in the project believe that the Bible is the Word of God - given to us in order that people might discover him and his purposes for our lives. We believe that the sixty-six books which go to make up the Bible, although written by different people, in different places, at different times, through different circumstances, have a single unifying theme: that theme is Salvation. This means free forgiveness and the removal of all our guilt, it means the gift of eternal life and it means the wholeness of purpose and joy which God has designed us to experience here and now, all this being possible through the Lord Jesus Christ.

How to use your Baker Bible Guide

These guides have been prepared both for personal study and for the leaders and members of small groups. More information about group study follows on the next few pages.

You can use this book very profitably as a personal study guide. The short studies are ideal for daily reading: the first of the following questions is usually aimed to help you with personal reflection (See *How to tackle personal Bible study*). If you prefer to settle down to a longer period of study you can use three to five studies at a time, and thus get a better overview of a longer Bible passage. In either case using the Bible Guide will help you to be disciplined about regular study, a habit that countless Christians have found greatly beneficial. (See also *How to tackle Timothy and Titus* for methods of selecting studies if you do not intend to use them all.)

Yet a third use for Baker Bible Guides is as a quarry for ideas for the busy Bible teacher, providing outlines and application for those giving talks or sermons or teaching children. You will need more than this book can offer of course, but the way the Bible text is broken down, comments offered and questions raised may well suggest directions to follow.

How to tackle personal Bible study

We have already suggested that you might use this book as a personal study guide. Now for some more detail.

One of the best methods of Bible study is to read the text through carefully several times, possibly using different versions or translations. Having reflected on the material it is a good discipline to write down your own thoughts before doing anything else. At this stage the introduction of other books can be useful. If you are using this book as your main study resource, then read through the relevant sections carefully, turning up the Bible references that are mentioned. The questions at the end of each chapter are specifically designed to help you to apply the passage to your own situation. You may find it helpful to write your answers to the questions in your notes.

It is a good habit to conclude with prayer, bringing before God the things you have learned.

If this kind of in-depth study is too demanding for you and you have only a short time at your disposal, read the Bible passage, read the comments in the Bible Guide, think round one of the questions and commit what you have learned to God in a brief prayer. This would take about fifteen minutes without rushing it.

How to tackle your group Bible study

This guide is a commentary on God's word, written to help a group to get the most out of their studies. Although it is never ideal to chop up Scripture into small pieces, which the authors never intended, huge chunks are indigestible and we have tried to provide a diet of bite-sized mouthfuls.

If you want to get an overview of the Bible book in a series of meetings you will need to select appropriate studies for each meeting. Read them yourself first and prepare a short summary of the studies you are tackling for your group. Ideally you could write it on a sheet of A5 and hand a copy to each member.

Do not attempt to pack more than one study into one meeting but choose the crucial one which best crystallizes the message. There are examples in *How to tackle Timothy and Titus* below.

1. Resources

You will find any or all of the following books of great value in providing background to your Bible knowledge. Put some of them on your Christmas list and build up your library.

Atlas of the Bible and Christianity (Baker).
Evangelical Commentary on the Bible (Baker).
Baker's Bible Handbook (Baker).
Evangelical Dictionary of Biblical Theology (Baker).
NIV Study Bible (Zondervan).

The relevant volume in the IVP Tyndale Commentary series will give you reliable and detailed help with any knotty points you may encounter.

2. Preparing to lead

Reading, discussing with friends, studying, praying, reflecting on life ... preparation can be endless. But do not be daunted by that. If you wait to become the perfect leader you will never start at all. The really vital elements in preparation are:

▶ prayer (not only in words but an attitude of dependence on God, 'Lord, I can't manage this on my own')

▶ familiarity with the study passage (careful reading of the text, the Bible Guide study and any other resource books that throw light on it) and

▶ a clear idea of where you hope to get in the meeting (notes on your introduction, perhaps, recap what was covered at the last meeting, and what direction you hope the questions will take you in – don't force the group to give your answers).

Here is a short checklist for the busy group leader.

Have I prayed about the meeting?

Have I decided exactly what I want to achieve through the meeting?

Have I prepared the material?

Am I clear about the questions that will encourage positive group discussion?

Am I gently encouraging silent members?

Am I, again gently, quietening the chatterers?

Am I willing to admit ignorance?

Am I willing to listen to what the group says and to value their contributions?

Am I ready not to be dogmatic, not imposing my ideas on the group?

Have I planned how to involve the group in discovering for themselves?

Have I developed several 'prayer points' that will help focus the group?

Are we applying Scripture to our experience of real life or only using it as a peg to hang our opinions on?

Are we finding resources for action and change or just having a nice talk?

Are we all enjoying the experience together?

How to tackle Timothy and Titus

Now let's assume that you are planning an eight-week course of studies (you will have to make the adjustments if you have more or fewer meetings). Where do you begin? This is entirely up to you and your group of course but, to get you started, here are four possible routes you might take.

1. Focus on one book

Make an in-depth study of Paul's letter to Titus. It so happens that there are exactly eight studies on Titus in this book so selection is unnecessary. You may need, however, to extend 2:1–8 into the following week as it is very full and 2:9–10 on slavery may not give you enough material for a whole study.

2. 'Top selection'

To get an overview of Paul's two letters to Timothy select eight studies which will give you the essence of what he is writing about. How about:

1 Timothy 1:3–7	1 Timothy 6:3–10
1 Timothy 2:1–7	2 Timothy 2:3–7
1 Timothy 3:1–7	2 Timothy 3:14–17
1 Timothy 4:1–5	2 Timothy 4:14–18

3. Pursue a theme

A major theme in these letters is the Christian church's conflict with false teaching. Use the Contents (pp. 5–8) and select a series on this topic.

Alternatively look at Paul's encouragement to Timothy and Titus to committed, hard-working discipleship. Eight studies on this theme might well feature:

1 Timothy 1:12–17	2 Timothy 1:6–7
1 Timothy 3:8–13	2 Timothy 2:3–7
1 Timothy 6:11–16	2 Timothy 4:1–4
Titus 3:1–8a	2 Timothy 4:5–8

4. Tackle the tough one

For us today the most controversial subject of these letters (especially in 1 Timothy) is Paul's view of women's roles in the church. The author of this guide believes that Christians have often misunderstood Paul at this point. If you want to get your teeth into this one, here are eight studies:

1 Timothy 2:8–10	1 Timothy 5:6, 11–16
1 Timothy 2:11–12	Titus 2:1–8
1 Timothy 2:13–15	2 Timothy 2:3–7
1 Timothy 3:8–13	2 Timothy 3:1–9

These are not all the same 'weight' of course. 1 Timothy 2:11–12 is the crucial one and may need more than one session.

These outlines are meant to be springboards for your own ideas, so please do not follow them slavishly. Adapt them for your own use, merge them or ignore them.

In any case much of these letters will go unread if you concentrate only on these short snippets. You as leader will need to read carefully the whole of each letter, and will be able to refer your group to sections they have not read. It would be wise to read aloud a whole chapter whenever studying a part of it – the context often throws light on the verses you are looking at.

What can we expect to learn from Timothy and Titus?

All Scripture is God-breathed and is useful (2 Timothy 3:16).

So how can it be 'useful' to us in our church today?

► How to help inexperienced church members to become true disciples, fully equipped for the Lord's service, and motivated as committed soldiers, dedicated athletes and hardworking farmers living a life of beautiful deeds.

► In days when Christians still disagree with each other and churches divide, how can we recognize false teaching, obsession with non-essentials, legalism, aggressive attitudes, subtle intrusion of the occult, controversy that becomes divisive, and eliminate them all by means of true teaching.

► How can we understand difficult verses that have puzzled honest men and wounded gifted Christian women: and illumined by the Holy Spirit encourage both men and women in happy fruitful service together in our churches.

► How to confront difficult people and tackle tough situations, as Titus had to cope with the Cretans.

► How to detect and combat the creeping love of money

which can so easily motivate even church leaders and wreck their ministries.

▶ How to care for the different categories of needy people in the church, especially widows, but including young men and women, seniors who may feel left out, and those who are economically deprived in slavish labour.

▶ The missionary challenge of the lives and commitment of Paul, Timothy and Titus: the church today still needs workers like this.

A careful study of these three priceless letters will help us both as individuals and as congregations to discern what is important in our contemporary life and worship and what is not.

Finding your way round this book

In our Bible Guides we have developed special symbols to make things easier to follow. Every study therefore has an opening section which is the passage in a nutshell.

The main section is the one that *makes sense of the passage*.

Questions

Every passage also has special questions for personal and group study after the main section. Some questions are addressed to us as individuals, some speak to us as members of our church or home group, while others concern us as members of God's people worldwide. The questions are deliberately designed:

▶ to get people thinking about the passage

▶ to apply the text to 'real life' situations

▶ to encourage reflection, discussion and action!

As a group leader you may well discover additional questions that will have special relevance to your group, so look out for these and note them in your preparation time.

Digging deeper

Some passages, however, require an extra amount of explanation, and we have put these into two categories. The first kind gives additional background material that helps us to understand something factual. For example, if we dig deeper into the gospels, it helps us to know who the Pharisees were, so that we can see more easily why they related to Jesus in the way they did. These background sections are marked with a spade.

Important doctrines

The second kind of explanatory section appears with passages which have important doctrines contained in them and which we need to study in more depth if we are to grow as Christians. Special sections that explain them to us in greater detail are marked with a face as above.

Chronology of St Paul's life

Date	Christian history	Roman history
c. 28–30	**Jesus'** public ministry	14–37 **Tiberius** emperor
c. 33	Conversion of Saul	
c. 35	Paul's *first* post-conversion visit to Jerusalem	
35–46	Paul in Cilicia with *Barnabas* in **Antioch**	37–41 **Caligula** emperor 41–54 **Claudius** emperor
46	Paul's *second* visit to Jerusalem (famine visit)	
47–48	**First missionary journey** with *Barnabas* to Cyprus (2 cities) and to Galatia (5 cities) Return to **Antioch** (confronts Peter)	
48?	*Letter to the Galatians*	
49	**Council of Jerusalem** (*third* visit)	49 Jews expelled from Rome
49–50	**Second missionary journey** with *Silas* and *Timothy* through Anatolia to Macedonia (3 cities) and Greece (2 cities)	
50	*Letter to the Thessalonians*	
50–52	Paul in **Corinth** (two years)	51–52 *Gallio*, proconsul of Achaia

Timothy and Titus

Date	Christian history	Roman history
52 (Summer)	Paul's *fourth* Jerusalem visit Returned to *Antioch*	52–29 *Felix*, procurator of Judaea
52–55	**Third missionary journey** Paul in **Ephesus** (1 city for 3 years)	54–68 **Nero** emperor
55–56	*Letters to the Corinthians*	
55–57	Paul in Macedonia, Illyricum and Achaia	
57 (early)	*Letter to the Romans*	
57 (May)	Paul's *fifth* Jerusalem visit	
57–59	Paul imprisoned in Caesarea	59 *Festus* succeeds Felix as procurator of Judaea
59 (Sept)	**Paul's voyage to Rome begins**	
60 (Feb)	Paul arrives in **Rome**	
60–62	Paul under house arrest in **Rome**	
?60–62	*Captivity Letters*	62 *Festus* dies, succeeded by *Albinus*, as procurator
?62	**Paul released from Rome** (?) Visits **Ephesus**, finds error, leaves *Timothy* to clear up. Evangelizes Crete, leaves *Titus* Writes *1 Timothy, Titus*	
?63, 64	**Paul re-arrested in Ephesus** (?) taken to **Rome** Writes *2 Timothy* with Luke	64 Great Fire of Rome
?65	**Paul and Peter martyred** **in Rome**	
65–69	Mark and Luke writing *Gospels, Acts*	

Asia Minor in Paul's day

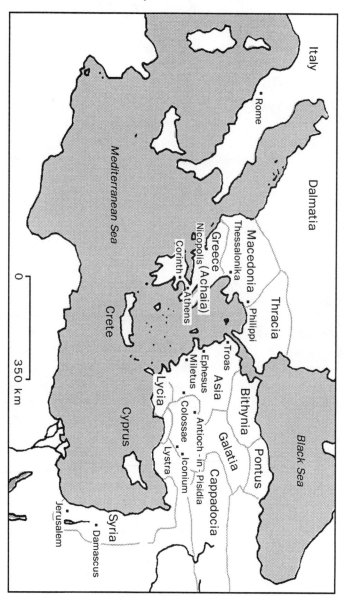

Asia Minor in the time of Paul

Introducing Paul's letters
to Timothy and Titus

We often think of Paul as author of a large part of the New Testament, but he was never a man who sat in a library cooking up theories: he was a militant activist with street credibility, engaged in vigorous evangelism and church planting. When he met a problem in the church, he would think about it, theologize and write to help churches sort out their problems. Archaeologists have dug up many ordinary letters written to individuals in the first century AD. However, letters written to encourage Christian churches are a new kind of writing, which Paul himself seems to have invented. While letters like Philippians or Corinthians were mostly addressed to whole congregations, we do have a few written to individuals like Philemon, and including these three letters we are going to look at together.

We will study these three letters, not in the order in which they come in the Bible, but in what seems to be the order in which they were written – 1 Timothy, Titus and then 2 Timothy. All three appear to have been written after Paul was set free from his first Roman imprisonment (Acts 28). Probably 1 Timothy and Titus were written around the same time, between AD 62 and 65, after Paul had visited Ephesus and Crete, while Paul was still at liberty. He must have written 2 Timothy from prison in Rome after being rearrested.

1 Timothy 1:1–2

Paul's greetings to Timothy

Paul's greetings turn into prayer.

 It can be quite thrilling to find an old letter in the back of a cupboard. It might be a hundred years old. Who wrote it and who was it written to? What does it say? Does it sound like what we would say today?

This letter of Paul's is not one hundred years old but more than nineteen hundred (though it would have helped a lot if Paul and the other apostles had dated their letters as Ezekiel dated his prophecies). At first sight it's obvious who wrote it (Paul) and to whom (Timothy). In those days letter writers announced who they were at the beginning and said something about themselves; then who they were writing to and a word or two of greeting. As with many of his letters, which we have in the New Testament, Paul follows the usual custom, but turns his greetings into a prayer for:

▶ *Grace*, God's supply of blessing and strength to Timothy (see 1 Corinthians 15:10)

▶ *Mercy*, God's undeserved forgiveness and constant loving care, towards Jews and Gentiles alike

▶ *Peace*, using the traditional Jewish greeting *Shalom*, not merely a feeling of quietness, but the reality of God's power and presence.

Here we have what appears to be a typical opening to one of Paul's letters. An ageing missionary teacher writes to a younger man who is to succeed him in church work. To us it seems quite natural for someone to write to another person, as indeed it was then, but Paul usually wrote to whole churches rather than individuals: to the church at Corinth, Philippi or Colosse. And then it seems odd that he tells Timothy that he is an apostle; your 'father in the faith' would fit better with calling Timothy his son (verse 2).

Danger: false teaching!

It is clear from verse 3 that Timothy was at Ephesus when he received this letter and it may be Paul was writing his 'second letter to the Ephesians', expecting the church to read it over Timothy's shoulder. Why did he not write directly to 'the church in Ephesus' as we might expect? Perhaps because Paul did not want the church elders there to get hold of it: they might have suppressed it! For Paul was writing about the dangers of false teaching and when he said farewell to those very leaders by the docks at Miletus, in a scene movingly described in Acts chapter 20, he told them that *from your own number men will arise and distort the truth* and lead astray the faithful (Acts 20:30). This may explain why this letter is not addressed to 'the church in Ephesus' or to its overseers and deacons (as in Philippians 1:1).

So we should read this as another letter to the Ephesian church, sent to them through Timothy. Probably Hymenaeus and Alexander (1:20) were such elders who had been put out of the church by Paul himself. The rules about elders and deacons (chapter 3) are not vague theory (in case you might want to appoint an elder), but point to present leaders who quarrel, love money, are sexually impure and cannot teach correctly.

Paul writes *by the command of God our Saviour* (verse 1), a standard phrase like 'by order' and used of royal commands. Although 'Saviour' is a common word among Christians today it comes only twenty-four times in the whole of the New Testament (ten in these Pastoral Letters). This may be because pagan rulers were called *saviours* of their people so the early church used it sparingly. It was associated with the Roman cult of emperor worship. Here, one greater than Caesar, the true King of kings, commands Paul to be his apostle and special envoy.

Christ Jesus our hope looks to God's great salvage operation when Jesus will come again to gather his people to himself.

Paul calls Timothy his *true son*, or 'legitimate son' (verse 2), words used also of Titus (Titus 1:4), referring not to their physical sonship but spiritual; Paul may well have led them to the faith, in the case of Timothy perhaps on his first visit to Lystra (2 Timothy 3:11). But the greetings are cut short, because Paul is impatient to come to the reason for his letter, to warn Timothy and the church at Ephesus of the danger of false teaching.

Questions

1. Imagine you are Timothy. Paul has asked you to draft a letter to young people who have just become Christians. What will you include in the letter?
2. How do your church leaders and members help each other to keep the true faith? How well are you working together?
3. How far should state rulers regard themselves as 'saviours'? How should we view them?

Why 'Pastoral' letters?

These three letters of Paul, two to Timothy and one to Titus, are usually called 'Pastoral' letters, though only for the last 300 years, and the Bible never calls them that. 'Pastoral' here does not mean anything to do with farming or the countryside (though farmers are mentioned in 2 Timothy 2:6). 'Pastor' originally meant shepherd, and the word has come to be applied to the Christian leader who cares for the flock or congregation. So these letters express Paul's pastoral care for the people.

They form a distinct group which seem to have been written at the end of Paul's life. They help us to understand how churches were run as they got into their stride. 1 Timothy and Titus appear to be intended to be read by congregations in Ephesus and Crete respectively, while 2 Timothy seems to be a personal letter to an individual.

Timothy: a mini-biography

The New Testament tells us a great deal about Paul's younger fellow-worker. It will help us if we summarize the information:

Early life, conversion and commissioning

Timothy learned the Scriptures from his grandmother, Lois, and his mother, Eunice (2 Timothy 1:5; 3:15). Paul made three visits to Timothy's house at Lystra (today just a big mound in modern central-south Turkey). On the first visit Paul was stoned and left for dead (Acts 14:6–20), but soon afterwards he returned and appointed elders for the young church (Acts 14:21–23).

Timothy saw Paul's sufferings and was converted (2 Timothy 3:10–11), was well-spoken of by the Christians in Lystra (Acts 16:2) and was chosen by Paul to accompany him on his missionary travels. Timothy was circumcised (Acts 16:3). He was commissioned by the laying on of hands by the elders and by Paul (1 Timothy 4:14; 2 Timothy 1:6).

Missionary travels

Timothy seems to have spent much of his time assisting Paul on his travels and acting as a follow-up man and troubleshooter. His movements can be summarized:

- ▶ he accompanied Paul and Silas on the 'second missionary journey' (Acts 16:3–4)
- ▶ stayed in Thessalonica (Acts 17:10)
- ▶ stayed on in Berea (Acts 17:14–15)
- ▶ went back to Thessalonica (1 Thessalonians 3:1–6)
- ▶ rejoined Paul in Corinth (Acts 18:5)
- ▶ was sent to Philippi (Philippians 2:19–23)
- ▶ went back to Corinth (Acts 19:22; 1 Corinthians 4:17; 16:10–11)
- ▶ in this letter we find that he was asked to remain in Ephesus (1 Timothy 1:3)
- ▶ he was called to bring Mark to Paul in Rome (2 Timothy 4:9, 21)
- ▶ he was imprisoned and released (Hebrews 13:23).

This is already a massive programme for a shy young man and it is clear that the New Testament records only part of his ministry.

Paul's visits to Ephesus

Ephesus had been an important port on the west coast of what is now Turkey (see map p. 21) and centre of the worship of the mother goddess Cybele, later replaced by Artemis (Diana). The cutting down of forests caused erosion and its harbour silted up,

27

so Ephesus lost its boast to be the 'gateway to Asia' on the major eastern trade routes. We hear more about the church of Ephesus than any other congregation in the New Testament. Paul's long-standing relationship with Christians in Asia Minor includes:

▶ A first 'stopover' recorded in Acts 18:18–21; accompanied by Aquila and Priscilla, he promises to return *if it is God's will.*

▶ Two-year mission (Acts 19:1 – 20:1). The gospel was preached widely and churches planted to the east (Colosse, Hierapolis and Laodicea) and the north of Ephesus (Smyrna, Pergamum, Thyatira, Sardis and Philadelphia).

▶ The 'Miletus conference' with the elders (Acts 20:16–38). Here he warned them that some of them would distort the truth (verses 19–30).

▶ Paul was arrested in Jerusalem and taken to Rome. Under house-arrest there he wrote letters to Ephesus, Colosse and to Philemon.

▶ Paul's recent visit (1 Timothy 1:3); after being freed from house-arrest in Rome he had hoped to go west, to Spain (Romans 15:24, 28), but instead he made for Colosse to visit Philemon (Philemon 22), going via Ephesus. His fears about false teaching were proved true and he had to put two heretics out of the church (verse 20).

When Paul wrote 1 Timothy and Titus, he seems to have expected to return to Ephesus again (1 Timothy 3:14). He was rearrested, however, and wrote his second letter to Timothy back in prison in Rome once again.

WARNING AGAINST
FALSE TEACHERS

1 Timothy 1:3b–20

1 Timothy 1:3b–7

Beware false teaching!

After greeting Timothy, Paul urges him to silence people giving false teaching and going overboard on exciting fancies at Ephesus.

Paul is deeply troubled and rushes at once into the main reason for his writing, omitting his usual extended prayer and thanksgiving (verse 3: compare Galatians 1:6, where he does the same thing, with Philippians 1:1–11, his more usual style).

Some people read Timothy (and the rest of the Bible) as though it were a hotchpotch of texts, odd thoughts strung together almost at random. But Paul is dealing with an actual situation of spiritual warfare and his argument flows strongly through the letter from start to finish. Verse 3 is the key that explains Paul's train of thought. Dealing with the crisis caused by false teaching is the single theme that ties the whole letter together.

When a young church is growing rapidly life is exciting. New Christians are daily learning new truths: the deep, deep love of God becomes a reality; the meaning of the cross and Jesus' sacrifice for us and the presence and power of the Holy Spirit can be almost intoxicating. Unfortunately these conditions are fertile ground for new untruths too. Excited, untaught, often young people take on board uncritically every new idea that is going; their appetite is whetted for more and more exciting 'advances' and leaders who produce the goods in the form of false teaching may well become very popular. This was the problem at Ephesus as Paul saw it and is the problem in many growing churches today.

False teaching versus the simple truth

False doctrines have been taught at Ephesus by church leaders: *certain men* (verse 3) means 'certain persons'. It includes, also, women false teachers; both men and women had been teaching error (see chapter 2). False teaching is the key which makes sense of the whole letter. Paul has withdrawn the authority of the elders (verse 3) and appointed Timothy instead who has been left behind to sort out the mess.

Paul trained his helpers (as Jesus had trained the Twelve) by letting them watch him in action and then sending them out to work on their own. Ephesus seems to have been Timothy's fourth solo assignment. Earlier he had been sent to Thessalonica in about AD 50, Corinth (about AD 53–54) and Philippi (about AD 60–62) (see p. 27).

The problem of false teaching was not confined to Ephesus. In Corinth they preached a *different gospel* (2 Corinthians 11:4) and in Galatia a *different Jesus* (Galatians 1:6). John's letters to the Seven churches (Revelation 2–3) show how widespread false teaching was in Asia Minor. This warning should help us to detect false teaching in our own churches. 'Different' teaching may be wrong!

This section contrasts the complications, shiftiness and meaninglessness of false teaching with the straightforwardness, simplicity and sincerity of the true.

▶ *God's work* (verse 4). God's arrangements for people's redemption are straightforward.

▶ *The goal of this command* (verse 5). Paul has ordered Timothy to stay in Ephesus.

▶ promote *love, which comes from a pure heart* (see Psalms 24:4; 51:10).

▶ a *good conscience*, awareness of what is right and wrong, and

▶ *sincere faith*, without playacting.

 Our teaching aims to help Christians to be truly integrated men and women in heart, conscience and faith.

Wanderers

Paul describes these false teachers as wanderers. They have *wandered away* (verse 6: see also 1 Timothy 6:21; 2 Timothy 2:18), leaving the straight path of Christian truth and turning off into *meaningless talk*. False teaching has its own meaningless jargon, or perhaps the gibberish is sinister and occult.

The false teachers aspire to great things, to be *teachers of the law* (verse 7), a respectful title when used of the great Gamaliel, who himself taught Paul the Law (Acts 5:34), but derisive of these Ephesians who have no authority for what they tell people so confidently. Persuasive talk does not necessarily spring from secure truth. In fact they don't know what they are talking about! Paul had spent years studying under Gamaliel and knew more about the law than these Ephesians ever would.

Questions

1. Collect what you have learned so far about the nature of the false teaching in Ephesus (there is more to come). What parallels can you see today?
2. How do you decide whether some novel idea is true or false? What action can we take to avoid being diverted from the church's true task by endless discussions on what we should believe?

3. Why does it matter what we believe? Won't God take care of us anyway? What beliefs are really necessary?

What was this false teaching in Ephesus?

Paul never spells it out for us (he was writing to Timothy and the Ephesians and they knew already), but we have plenty of clues. Acts 19:13–19 tells us that Ephesus was a hotbed of strange cults, many of them involved with the occult, and the church would be living in this atmosphere of 'New Age' teaching from the start.

- *Myths* (verse 4, also called *godless myths and old wives' tales* in 1 Timothy 4:7). This suggests that the new teaching was based on stories and ideas rather than facts, interpreted by experience.

- *Endless genealogies* (verse 4). The Jews loved to spend time debating their ancestry back to Adam and Eve (see the explanation on *Jewish myths in Titus 1:14* (p. 143) and the explanation of 1 Timothy 2:13).

- *Controversies* (verse 4). The RSV calls them 'speculations'. *God's work* involves loving people, telling them the Good News, healing, helping and building people up, not spending time in endless meetings for discussions of speculations.

- *Meaningless talk* (verse 6). Secret occult groups sometimes use gibberish to confuse outsiders. All groups, including our Christian fellowships, tend to use in-group jargon, incomprehensible to others and something for us all to beware of and avoid; for example, we use phrases such as 'seeking just to touch the lost ...', 'feel free to share ...', 'We lift before thee two Poles' *etc*.

33

▶ *The law* (verse 7). The false teachers stressed keeping the rules (see also Titus 3:9). This was a Jewish tendency and may have excluded Gentiles (non-Jews).

Where did this false teaching come from?

Error spreads almost as fast as the truth. Paul had travelled with Aquila and Priscilla from Corinth to Ephesus. While he was based in Ephesus the gospel spread up the Lycus valley to Colosse, Laodicea and Hierapolis. But if the gospel followed this route error could travel back the same way! We often talk as though each church had its own peculiar set of teachings, like 'the Colossian heresy', but the false teachings in Corinth, Colosse and Ephesus were quite similar (see p. 89).

This is obvious from the excavation of ancient sites where, over and over again, temples, statues and remains are found of the same cults and beliefs (Aphrodite / Venus; Dionysus/ Bacchus; Cybele/Artemis/Diana). The eastern trade routes that came through Ephesus brought Hindu and Buddhist concepts about the physical world. This resulted in a hotchpotch of 'religious spirituality' not unlike New Age teachings today. The new Gentile converts had grown up in a society soaked in such ideas.

✓False teaching may add to or take away from the truth. Medicine becomes useless either if it has poisonous substances added to it, or if essential ingredients are left out. Church teaching may be false, either because things are added (perhaps from superstitious folk beliefs), or because essential truths like human bias towards sin, the death and bodily resurrection of Jesus, or the work of the Holy Spirit are left out. The Pharisees *added* human traditions to God's revelation: The Sadducees *subtracted* belief in resurrection and angels.

1 Timothy 1:8-11

The purpose of the law

False teachers claimed to teach the law. Paul describes the true purpose of the law.

 A favourite phrase of Paul's is *we know* (verse 8: see, for instance, Romans 2:2; 8:28 and 1 Corinthians 8:1). He is beginning at a point of common knowledge, 'We all agree don't we?' The purpose of the law of Moses was to reveal sin and restrain evil (Romans 7:7). And the *law* must be used *lawfully* (Paul makes a play on words here), and not be used as material for guesswork. Law-abiding people don't even need to know the law. Adam didn't. Only baddies and lawyers need to know the difference between burglary and housebreaking! The law is for the wicked; to make clear where they're going wrong and to try and restrain their wickedness.

Paul now lists thirteen vices (others are listed in Romans 1:29–32; 1 Corinthians 5:10–11; Galatians 5:19–21) which seem to be based loosely on the Ten Commandments. The first six words are arranged in three pairs. It may help us to set them out like this:

1 Timothy 1:9–10	Exodus 20:3–17
1 Lawbreakers and rebels (verse 9)	The first commandment, *You shall have no other gods before me* (verse 3).

35

1 Timothy 1:9–10	Exodus 20:3–17
2 Ungodly and sinful (verse 9) Those who do not honour the Lord's name.	Third commandment, *You shall not misuse the name of the* LORD *your God* (verse 7).
3 Unholy and irreligious (verse 9) who do not keep any day holy at all.	Fourth commandment, *Remember the Sabbath day by keeping it holy* (verse 8).
4 Those who kill their fathers or mothers (verse 9). Even striking a parent was punishable by death in Israel (Exodus 21:15) and under Roman law.	Fifth commandment, *Honour your father and your mother* (verse 12).
5 Murderers (verse 9)	Sixth commandment, *You shall not murder* (verse 13).
6 Adulterers and perverts (verse 10)	Seventh commandment, *You shall not commit adultery* (verse 14). This means sinful acts, homosexual or heterosexual, which threaten marriage (see 1 Corinthians 6:9). The German word for adultery means 'pair-breaking'. Sexual orientation is not in itself sinful but neutral. In the Bible, all heterosexual or homosexual genital activity outside the exclusive one man/one woman relationship is seen as sinful.

1 Timothy 1:9–10	Exodus 20:3–17
7 Slave traders (verse 10) Stealing people (kidnapping) is meant by Paul (see Exodus 21:16; Deuteronomy 24:7).	Eighth commandment, *You shall not steal* (verse 15).
8 Liars and perjurers (verse 10)	Ninth commandment, *You shall not give false testimony* (verse 16). Telling untruths about others in a court of law or in human society generally.

Sound doctrine

In case Paul has left anything out he adds, *whatever else is contrary to the sound doctrine* (verse 10) showing that the hideous list he has given is not the end of it. These are just examples! Sound doctrine is an important phrase. It comes eight times in the Pastoral Letters. The Greek word translated 'sound' was a medical term, and from it we get our English word 'hygiene'. It is the opposite of 'sick and 'unhealthy' and was used of lame men becoming 'perfectly whole' (John 5:15; Acts 4:10); we could say 'healthy doctrine'. The law is for the morally diseased. The gospel is health-giving. Doctor Luke probably favoured this word and Paul may be imitating Greek philosophers who called their opponents 'sick in mind'. If the truth is being taught and learned and lived out in our churches we should see more and more healthy minds and wholesome lives. Error produces the opposite.

In verse 11 (and in 6:15) God is called *blessed*, the source of all blessing. Paul is about to tell us how he has experienced this blessing for himself and he prepares us by reminding us that God has entrusted the gospel to him.

37

Questions

---

1. How can we best 'use the law'? How can we encourage each other so that the Scriptures turn us away from sin?
2. In what ways are Christians today tempted to be 'liars and perjurers'? Think of your relationship both with fellow-Christians and also unbelievers. Is it possible to live a lie without actually telling one?
3. How would a person with homosexual orientation react to this section? Explain the Christian view of lifelong relationship between one man and one woman (see Matthew 19:3–6).

1 Timothy 1:12–17

Paul tells how God revolutionized his life

Paul's own life is living proof of God's patience towards a proud, blaspheming, persecuting sinner who acted in ignorance and unbelief.

A living witness

Paul never misses a chance to give his testimony, to tell his readers what God has done for him (verse 12). It looks as if he is straying from his point but this is not so. The false teachers were insisting that obeying the law of Moses was essential. But Paul had been a teacher of the law, before God in Christ had called him, and he knew that it could not save him. When he turned to Christ at his conversion, he received mercy from God (verses 13 and 16) and grace (verse 14), not law. As a drowning person cannot save himself by thrashing more and more wildly about, so Paul, the Ephesians and all of us need the grace and mercy of God lovingly to rescue us. The law has no power to save us.

Paul is so excited by this thought that he bursts into a spontaneous 'doxology' or shout of praise (verse 17). This often happens in Paul's letters (see for instance Romans 11:33–36; 16:27; Galatians 1:5; Ephesians 3:20; 1 Timothy 6:15). Perhaps, like Paul, we should pause at this point to break into praise and to thank the invisible, eternal King for saving each of us.

Paul's violent attacks on the church, before his conversion, were so vicious that Luke had likened him to a wild beast (Acts 8:1, 3; 9:1–2; 26:9–11); Paul admits here that he had been a violent, proud, insolent bully (verse 13). Today, people like Paul are no more out of the reach of God's mercy than Paul was. We need to pray for them.

An aspect of God's loving-kindness comes in here. Paul had acted 'in ignorance and unbelief' (verse 13) and he knew that God understood that. Like all religious persecutors Paul thought he was serving God, not sinning against him. The Old Testament notes the difference between deliberate sins (see, for example, Psalm 19:13) and unintentional ones (Numbers 15:22–31 explains it all). Both Jesus and Stephen prayed for those who killed them. Paul had been present at the stoning of Stephen and the martyr's prayer was answered (Acts 7:59 – 8:1).

Jesus came into the world to rescue those who have gone wrong

Paul loved inventing new words, adding a prefix to strengthen what he wanted to say (as in our word 'hyper-active'). Here he calls the grace of God 'superabundantly-bestowed' on him (verse 14: Amplified Bible); poured out recklessly. Brutal, cynical, fanatical Paul was transformed *by the faith and love that are in* (that is 'by means of') *Christ Jesus*. It was not just that Paul changed sides but that the Lord changed Paul's nasty nature as well. The false teachers of the law have turned away from faith and love (verse 6), they blaspheme (verse 20) and engage in malicious quarrelling (6:4), all the things that Paul had been saved from.

In verse 15 we have the first of the five *trustworthy sayings* that appear in these letters (see p. 41): *Christ Jesus came into the world to save sinners*. This sentence contains two fundamental Christian truths; the 'incarnation' (*came into the world*) and 'redemption' (*to save sinners*).

▶ The Christ who had always existed 'came into' the world from outside to save it. Christmas celebrates the physical birth of Jesus but he had always existed as the eternal Son of God.

▶ He came to save sinners of whom, Paul adds, *I am the worst* (the first, the foremost). Some Christians have argued that we should think of ourselves as no longer sinners now we are saved by faith. But Paul does not say, 'I was', but 'I am' the worst. We were sinners when we were saved and we are still sinners now with an ever-present Saviour. I needed him then and I still need him now.

God had chosen Paul of all people, a 'worst case', a bully and persecutor, to be a prototype or example to the rest of us (verse 16). If Paul could receive mercy so can anybody!

Questions

1. Have we become too used to being saved? How can we keep alive and fresh our gratitude to God for his grace?
2. What can we learn from Paul's testimony how to draw people's attention to God, not to ourselves (see also Acts 21:1–21; 26:4–18)?

3. How can we help a world governed by greed and market forces to see that God's grace matters more than human achievement?

The five 'trustworthy sayings'

Five times in these Pastoral Letters Paul uses the phrase, 'This (or 'here') is a trustworthy saying'. The trustworthy saying in 2 Timothy 2:11 has the rhythm of a hymn. It may well be that Paul is quoting well-known words from hymns, spiritual songs or church prayers. Here are the five:

▶ *Christ Jesus came into the world to save sinners* (1 Timothy 1:15).

▶ *If anyone sets his heart on being an overseer, he desires a noble task* (1 Timothy 3:1).

▶ *We have put our hope in the living God, who is the Saviour of all, and especially of those who believe* (1 Timothy 4:9–10).

▶ *If we died with him, we will also live with him; if we endure, we will also reign with him* (2 Timothy 2:11–13).

▶ *Having been justified by his grace, we might become heirs having the hope of eternal life* (Titus 3:7–8).

1 Timothy 1:18–20

Back to the problem of false teaching

**Paul returns to his instructions, focusing
on two men, false teachers who had been
put out of the church. Spiritual leadership
is a battle which can be tragically lost.**

After his joyful outburst (verse 17) Paul
wrenches himself back to the main purpose
of his letter and he repeats the address
Timothy, my son and the *instruction* (or
command, verses 3 and 5): 'Now, my boy, this is what you have
to do.'

Even now Paul does not 'pull rank' as an apostle or even as
Timothy's spiritual father, but reminds him that he, Timothy,
has a spiritual reputation to live up to. Prophecies had been
made about him. Exactly what they were or when they were
made is not clear. Paul may be referring to the 'prophetic
message when the body of elders laid their hands on you' (1
Timothy 4:14). He may also have had in mind that the 'brothers
at Lystra and Iconium spoke well of him' (Acts 16:2). This might
mean no more than that they gave him a good reference but it
could mean that at Timothy's commissioning service, Christians
from his home town, Lystra, and from Iconium, 40 kilometres
away, prophesied about his future service and usefulness.

Timothy knew then that he was expected to 'fight the good fight', 'war the beautiful warfare', the battle against false teaching that twists the gospel. The military picture is typical of Paul, struggling against opponents of the gospel. 'Spiritual warfare' is not only terrifying encounters with personal evil and occult power, but also an ongoing battle for biblical truth (Jude 3); a much less glamorous but perhaps even more necessary field of warfare. Failure to fight that battle may result in the shipwreck of faith (naval battles are just as important as those on land!) and two Ephesians in particular had gone that way, losing both faith and personal integrity.

Handed over to Satan

Who are these two people whom Paul has *handed over to Satan* and why does Paul name them? They are probably former elders of the Ephesian church, the men 'from your own number' of whom Paul had already warned the whole group of elders (Acts 20:30). This could have been a prophetic warning by Paul, though Luke, writing Acts after the event, may have known already what had happened.

The name Hymenaeus (verse 20) appears again in 2 Timothy 2:17, where he is described as having 'wandered away from the truth', by claiming that the resurrection has already taken place and thereby destroying some people's faith. Presumably he was claiming that Christians are already in heaven and will never die, but this is not clear.

Alexander (verse 20) may be the metalworker who did Paul 'a great deal of harm' (2 Timothy 4:14–15) and who strongly opposed the apostles' message; or he may be the Ephesian Jew of Acts 19:33. Perhaps the same man is referred to in all three places. Both false teachers had been 'delivered over to Satan', which means that Paul had put them out of the church. The same phrase is used in 1 Corinthians 5:1–5 and 2 Thessalonians 3:14–15 has a similar intent.

All these cases express the same purpose and hope, that the

people concerned will be reformed, will return and will be restored. There is no vindictiveness or punishment implied, only the hope of improvement. It was meant to be a temporary measure, until the sinner repented, and was aimed at their full recovery.

In our churches today practice varies. In some fellowships discipline is very strict and church members are given direction in quite mundane matters, while in other churches discipline is unheard of and members politely ignore each other's failings (in public at least – and make a meal of gossip about them in private!).

We have returned to the central theme of false teaching. Remember that the chapter divisions in our English Bibles were not put into Paul's letters until they were devised in the thirteenth century by Stephen Langton (whose name appears in the Magna Carta). So we may expect to see this train of thought about 'false teaching' continuing into the next chapter.

Questions

1. What are the root causes of wandering away from the faith, which result in faith-shipwreck?
2. Does your church impose too much or too little discipline? In what sort of matters should it have authority over the members and what should be left to individual conscience? Look for biblical principles in Matthew 7:1–6; 23:23–24; 1 Corinthians 5:9–13; 2 Corinthians 2:5–11; John 8:1–11.
3. How do you think that church leaders who fall into sin and 'make shipwreck' should be pastored: whose job is it?

CURRENT ERRORS EXPLORED

1 Timothy 2:1–15

1 Timothy 2:1–7

Prayer should be offered for everyone

Pray for the government! God wants us all to live in peace and have the means of knowing the truth in Christ.

The word, *then*, in verse 1 shows that what follows ties in with what has been said in chapter 1.

False teachers are usually exclusive, that is, they call together a group of 'special' people, the 'in-group' and exclude others who are not exactly likeminded. True Christianity is not like that. It is for everyone. That is why Paul repeats the word *all* three times. Prayer should be made for all persons (verse 1); God desires all to be saved (verse 4) and Jesus gave his life for all people (verse 6). The same idea appears in Paul's letter to nearby Colosse, 'teaching *everyone* with all wisdom so that we may present *everyone* perfect in Christ' (Colossians 1:28). It is hard for human beings, even Christians, to accept all other human beings as equally loved and favoured by God. In this context, it may have been Jewish believers, finding it hard to accept Gentile Christians. Some North American Indians called themselves 'human beings' to distinguish themselves from the 'palefaces'. We too may think of ourselves as special people, not like those pagan outsiders. If so, beware.

All kinds of prayer (as described in verse 1) should be made for all kinds of people, whether they are Christians or not. *First of all* means 'of first importance.' We need to pray for everyone but especially 'kings' (governors, rulers, magistrates, in fact, all who are in authority). The Jews set an example in the Old Testament, praying for a pagan government, even when it was oppressive (Jeremiah 29:7). Why should we follow their example? Paul gives four good reasons.

1. The first is practical: *that we may live peaceful and quiet lives in all godliness and holiness* (verse 2). If rulers have no reason to suspect Christians of being disloyal, they will be able to practise their faith without state interference. The peace established by the Romans over a huge area made it possible for Christians to take the gospel across the frontiers with greater freedom even than we enjoy today. In any case peace is a benefit to everyone, Christian or not, so we should pray for it. The word 'godliness', a word used only by Paul, comes eight times in these three letters. Paul may be borrowing a buzz word of the false teachers (as he does with 'wisdom' and 'knowledge' in 1 Corinthians 1–3 and 8:1–7). Paul used it to mean 'true Christianity'.

2. The second reason that we should pray for everyone is that *it is good, and pleases God our Saviour* (verse 3), reflecting the generous character of the One God. 'Saviour' was the common title given to emperors since Ptolemy I of Egypt and Paul might have been pointing out that earthly rulers were all doing God's will by protecting their people. Perhaps he intends to contrast earthly rulers who we have prayed *for* and the heavenly Saviour we pray *to*.

3. The third reason that we should pray for everyone is that God desires to bless them through the gospel. *God ... wants all human beings to be saved* (verse 3) might mean merely that God's nature is to promote the welfare of mankind. But Paul adds the words, *and come to a knowledge of the truth*. So salvation is more than welfare and common grace; it means being saved from sin, death and judgment.

47

Notice that God *wants* all this for people, but the word used here is not as strong as *wills*. God wants us to be saved but does not decree that we must be (see *God's will* ... p. 49).

4. The fourth reason for our prayer is the ransom paid by Christ, the one mediator (verses 5 and 6). The fact that he sacrificed himself for us is a strong motive for mission and evangelism. If my Lord desires everyone to be saved and come to a knowledge of the truth then so should I, and so should we, working together in committing our lives to our Lord's will. Paul has done this, as he tell us in verse 7.

A statement of faith

These verses sound like an extract from a creed, containing four compact, balanced, rhythmical phrases (1 Corinthians 8:6 is similar).

There is one God

Deuteronomy 6:4–9 (the 'Shema', which Jews repeat daily) and verse 5 here are vital to Christian belief. There are not three gods but one God and therefore one gospel (Romans 3:29–30). This is important to remember when we discuss our faith with Jews or Muslims: some of them accuse Christians of believing in three gods. If there were many gods, there would be many gospels. Religious pluralism offers us a supermarket of religions which are all relatively true. This is manifestly nonsense. There is only one God, and only one gospel (Romans 3:29–30).

Also one mediator

The middleman or go-between is the bridge person. Jesus is the bridge between God and humanity, himself both God and man. False teaching often loves to invent extra mediators: Moses (Galatians 3:19–20), angels (Hebrews 2:2), supernatural powers, saints, the Virgin Mary, Muhammad and (in these days of exposure to Asian monistic religions in schools) Hindu avatars

48

and Buddhist Bodhisattvas. If anyone or anything comes between us and God, except Jesus Christ our one mediator, something has gone wrong: we should suspect error.

He gave himself as a ransom for all

A ransom means an exchange price paid to set a slave free. Jesus used the word of himself (Mark 10:45; Matthew 20:28). His life was worth more than all creatures put together so his death provides enough ransom to set us all free, not just the few specially chosen elite.

The testimony given in its proper time

Everyone finds this phrase in verse 6 difficult. The idea of the *proper time* is repeated in 1 Timothy 6:15 and Titus 1:3. Perhaps it means 'The time that God knows to be the right one', the decisive moment in history.

Questions

1. In your times of prayer do you pray for *all* people or just a chosen few? How can you broaden your concern? (Use a newspaper, missionary newsletters, letters from friends etc.)
2. Does your church actively support the government, national and local? How could it improve in the light of verses 2 and 3 above?
3. Is government always to be obeyed? What happens when Christians are forbidden to meet, teach or practise their faith?

God's will and human disobedience

Can God be frustrated in getting what he wants? Some passages seem to answer 'No' to this. For instance, Job finally comes to the conclusion that … 'You can do all things; no plan of yours can be thwarted' (Job 42:2). In Islam this idea of the 'inthwartability' of God becomes a fundamental principle: he determines the whole of history, and our individual lives. But the God of the Bible is different. In Job great emphasis is laid by God himself on Job's free response to his sufferings – either to 'curse God and die' (Job 2:9) or to maintain his spiritual integrity. In fact, Scripture shows us a God who longs for his people to repent: 'All day long I have held out my hands to an obstinate people' (Isaiah 65:2).

So it seems that God has chosen to limit himself, refusing to overrule us when we reject him. But surely if he is God he can arrange things so that we have free will *and* he gets his own way too. This is like the problem of the little girl who asked, 'If God can do anything can he make a stone so heavy that he cannot lift it?' Our understanding runs dry at this point. Surely either our choice has some meaning or we have no power of choice at all, just a tantalizing pretence.

The New Testament apostles treat human beings as if they are able to respond, to accept or refuse the gospel. So it does seem as if God gives us the freedom to repent and believe or to remain hostile. He has made us 'in his image' and it seems that he respects us, not as his equals to be sure, but as responsible persons.

The motive for mission

Paul's call is based on God's character. The logic continues: if this is what God is like, and what Jesus is like, then small wonder that he has appointed me, Paul, as a missionary to fulfil his purpose. This is what ought to motivate us today to engage in mission. *For this* (*i.e.* to spread abroad this gospel) *I was appointed a herald and apostle* (1 Timothy 2:7). A herald declares with authority royal news that people have not heard before, so means the same as 'evangelist' But why does Paul say *I am*

telling the truth, I am not lying (see Romans 9:1; 2 Corinthians 11:31)? In view of the stress on 'all human beings' (verse 4), Paul is probably responding to Jewish doubts as to whether he should be winning Gentiles and baptizing them without circumcising them first. 'A teacher of the nations' (NIV – Gentiles): 'nations' corresponds to 'all persons', that the one God and the one mediator desire to be saved. Notice that herald, apostle and teacher describe the spiritual gifts needed for the three successive stages of missionary work – evangelistic preaching, apostolic church-planting and the teaching of disciples.

1 Timothy 2:8–10

Men and women at worship

When they pray together men must avoid anger and argument; women must not dress to attract notice.

Verse 8 begins with the word 'therefore' (omitted in the NIV) so Paul is obviously continuing his discussion, presumably from where he left off in verse 1. All kinds of prayer must be made for all kinds of people, so this is how it should be done and how it should not be done.

The men

Everywhere is more likely to mean 'among all the nations' rather than 'in every house church in Ephesus'. Paul seems to be echoing Malachi 1:11 here (as he does also in a prayer context in 1 Corinthians 1:2; 2 Corinthians 2:14; 1 Thessalonians 1:8). When

Gentiles start praying to the Lord it shows that Malachi's prophecy is being fulfilled. Wherever they gather to pray, however, men should be careful to come in the right frame of mind. It is easy just to turn up at church services or prayer meetings with no thought about making a positive contribution or, on the other hand, even bring some ill feeling that might poison the atmosphere of worship or torpedo the whole purpose of coming together to pray.

Positively, men are called upon to *lift up holy hands in prayer*. The only other New Testament reference to this custom is Jesus lifting his hands to bless (Luke 24:50). There are, however, Old Testament verses referring to this Jewish practice (for instance, 1 Kings 8:54; Psalm 63:4), but this does not mean that we must necessarily do the same today. The important emphasis is upon *holy* hands (see for instance, Psalm 24:3–4 and Isaiah 1:15). 'Hands stained with blood' as Isaiah points out, must not be raised in prayer and if they are, God will not listen. Hands or eyes raised to heaven, or knees bowed to the ground will not impress our God who knows our hearts, if we are full of bitterness, pride or unresolved anger. There were such arguments and disputes in Ephesus as we know from 1 Timothy 1:4; 3:3; 6:4. Jesus taught that when we come to pray we should first make our peace with others (Matthew 5:23, 24).

The women

Are the men to do the praying while the women concentrate on dressing properly? Not at all. There is a word meaning 'likewise' which begins verse 9 and is left out by the NIV translation. The argument, then, is '*As* the men should pray this way *so also* the women should pray as follows ...' They are engaged in worship (verse 10b). In the Bible, women's prayer is no less valuable than men's. Hannah's prayer is recorded at length (1 Samuel 2:1–10), so is Mary's (Luke 1:46–55); the women and Mary, the mother of Jesus, were among those praying in Jerusalem (Acts 1:14) and the first Christians in

Europe came from the praying group of women at Philippi (Acts 16:13).

We know from inscriptions that several Jewish women were leaders of synagogues in Asia Minor in the first century so there is no cultural problem about them praying, but there is a warning to them here. It is not about what they say or how they say it, but about how they dress. So it's obvious that they were taking part in public activity, being seen by others, or their manner of dress wouldn't have mattered. Flashy dressing in public was seen as a sign of marital unfaithfulness in Greek and Roman culture (see p. 55). So Christians at worship should be careful to avoid such appearances.

In any case sensational female dressing might well distract the men at the prayer meeting! The Amish Christians in Pennsylvania still stress the importance of 'dressing plain', as did the Quakers and Puritans in England. In these days of sexual freedom and so-called 'broadmindedness' such modesty may be regarded as hilariously old-fashioned, especially by the young. But Paul and Peter advised modest dress precisely because the society he and the Ephesians lived in was notoriously permissive. That permissiveness easily invades the church so that our standards imitate those of the pagan world outside. In the extremely permissive Roman society a woman could show she was chaste and faithful by modesty of dress. The Muslim solution to the same problem is to cover women completely. Jewish Christians in Ephesus would have been more conservative in dress than Gentiles. Women and girls today might pause, to ask themselves exactly why they are choosing to wear what they do to church or prayer meetings and whether they would choose differently if they knew that no men or boys would be present! And perhaps the same question should be asked of men too!

Get the priorities right

The baseline message is about nonverbal communication: that a young woman's public appearance at worship should not be 'look at me, how attractive I am', but 'look at God, how attractive he is', and this is achieved not by looking pretty but by doing good deeds. Dorcas 'was always doing good and helping the poor' (Acts 9:36). The story of the wisdom and kindness of Abigail back in Old Testament times is told in 1 Samuel 25. These and other examples of women doing good do not suggest that men should not do good as well ('oh, I leave all that church-going and do-goodery to the wife', you may have heard), nor that women should purposely dress shabbily, but that we should all get our priorities right. Even the organizers of the old-style beauty contests tried to show that entrants had more than vital statistics by interviewing them about their hobbies, aspirations and contribution to society.

Paul says that good deeds are the best way to make a woman attractive. Beauty can be skin deep while true kindness never is.

Questions

1. How can you improve your approach to public worship (1) in your attitude and preparation and (2) in what you choose to wear? (These apply both to men and women).
2. What can we learn about prayer in the early church from this passage? How does it apply to us?
3. Paul wrote in a particular cultural situation. What are the principles behind what he wrote and how do they apply to us in equally permissive societies?

Women in Greek, Roman and Jewish culture

To dress up and display one's physical charms in public usually implied marital unfaithfulness.

> A woman who likes adornment is not faithful.
> (Sextus, a Greek philosopher)

> There is nothing that a woman will not permit herself to do, nothing that she deems shameful, when she encircles her neck with green emeralds and fastens huge pearls to her elongated ears … so important is the business of beautification; so numerous are the piles and storeys piled upon one another on her head – meanwhile she pays no attention to her husband.
> (Juvenal, a Roman satirist)

Back in Old Testament times Isaiah had pronounced God's displeasure on just such over-dressing:

> In that day the Lord will snatch away their finery: the bangles and headbands and crescent necklaces, the ear-rings and bracelets and veils, the head-dresses and ankle chains and sashes, the perfume bottles and charms, the signet rings and nose rings, the fine robes and the capes and cloaks, the purses and mirrors, and the linen garments and tiaras and shawls.
> (Isaiah 3:18–23)

1 Timothy 2:11–12

Muzzle the female false teachers!

Women are to be instructed, and must not be allowed to go on teaching errors.

The meaning of verses 11–12 is among the most hotly contested of the whole Bible. In recent years men and women have argued bitterly about their respective roles both in  society and in the churches. There is nothing new about this for both William and Catherine Booth (founders of the Salvation Army) discuss these verses when commending women's ministry in the 19th century. It will not be surprising if it takes us some time to unravel the meaning of this passage, while we examine several possible interpretations. First of all there are four things to note about verse 11.

1. *A woman should learn.* 'A woman', of course, means 'women' here. Before we accuse Paul of condescension remember that 'learner' means 'disciple'. Some rabbis said women were not able to learn and questioned the wisdom of even letting them try. Jewish Christians in Ephesus had no cultural tradition of women studying, let alone teaching. Jesus changed all that, allowing Mary of Bethany to sit at his feet and be taught (Luke 10:38–42). There were women among the disciples of the Lord

(Luke 8:2–3) and Tabitha is described as 'a disciple' (Acts 9:36).

2. *In silence.* Why? The word in Greek is the same as that in verse 2 meaning 'quietness' (it cannot possibly mean 'silent lives'!). It may be a warning to avoid the excesses of the pagan female cults of Cybele and Dionysus, where women swayed their bodies with frenzied shrieks, howls and cries! Now that pagan women have become Christians, they must not import noisy pagan practices into the church. One cannot help wondering whether some of our worship today borders on that and what Paul might think. So not only Christian women's dress, but their demeanour too must be different from that of pagan women.

3. Paul is conscious of the danger of division between Jewish and Gentile culture. Possibly, intelligent Gentile women converts, without much background in the Scriptures, were attempting to teach before they had taken the trouble to learn. Paul tells them to learn first before presuming to teach. The Jews did not allow their women to teach publically, so one can imagine the Jewish Christian male reaction to Gentile Christian women wanting to teach in churches!

4. *Full submission.* Does this mean women saying 'Yes, Sir. Of course, sir' to everything a man may choose to say? Does the Bible teach the submission of all women, however wise and biblically instructed, to all men, however thick and clueless? Or only voluntary submission to one man, who loves them and is ready to sacrifice for them (Ephesians 5:25)? The same word is used in Ephesians 5:21 of all Christians submitting to one another, so it cannot carry the idea of grovelling 'kowtowing', as some have thought. It probably means 'in a proper relationship'. A similar word used by Greek military writers means 'rear deployment', that is, when lightly armed assault troops take up battle stations behind a phalanx of heavily armed infantry. They are equally important: neither unit is superior or inferior to the

other, but they have differing roles to play. Thus, before the famous passage on spiritual warfare in Ephesians 6 we read, translating freely, 'all of you take up your battle stations in relation to one another' (Ephesians 5:21). Specifically addressed to wives, it means 'Take up your position in relation to your own husband'.

The notorious verse 12

It is certainly notoriously difficult! Many devoted Christian women have been hurt by those who assert dogmatically that it means that no woman should ever teach men at any time, in any place or on any subject, because 'such activity would violate the structure of created sexual relationships', involving women in things for which they are not suited. Does Paul mean us to take this verse as an outright ban on any woman ever teaching on any subject at any time in any place? Paul himself does not seem to think so.

In his second letter, addressed to Timothy in the same city, Paul commands him to pass on what he has learned to 'faithful persons, who can teach others also' (2 Timothy 2:2). The original word sometimes refers to males (1 Corinthians 7:1; Ephesians 5:31), but its basic meaning is 'human person'. Had Paul meant what some are asserting he could have chosen the quite unambiguous Greek word for 'males' which he does not. In other words, Paul does not seem to understand himself to have imposed a permanent and universal ban in his first letter! Far from *condemning* women's ministry, Paul *commends* women's ministry in Romans 16 and Philippians 4:3 and *commands* it in 2 Timothy 2:2.

Please note well, that what is at issue here is not trying to evade this verse because it runs contrary to contemporary feminism, but because a high view of Scripture requires that Paul must be consistent with himself, and that Scripture must harmonize with Scripture.

A great deal has been written about this puzzle and a number of solutions offered which are outlined in *Interpreting verse 12* below. My own views have been influenced by the excellent teaching outlines produced by women students in sermon classes in both Britain and Canada. I incline to a combination of these solutions as follows: Paul's immediate practical purpose is to silence false teaching. Having kicked out two men himself, he tells Timothy to silence women false teachers. This was never intended as a ban on women ever teaching anywhere, but as a local stop-gap measure to solve an immediate problem (like getting them remarried, see 5:14). The *immediate* context is important, for Paul goes on to refute three cardinal errors of the false teaching about women (see verses 13–15 below). The Kroegers' researches (see below) make sense of the context in a way the traditional negative ban on women teaching never has. The *overall* context of the letter, that it is aimed at silencing false teachers, is decisive.

Note F. F. Bruce's helpful comment on this very passage. 'In general where there are divided opinions about the interpretation of a Pauline passage, that interpretation which runs along the line of liberty is much more likely to be true to Paul's intention than one which smacks of bondage or legalism'. And that bit of Aberdonian commonsense surely helps us see straight!

Questions

1. Read the solutions offered to solve the problem of verse 12 below. Which do you find most helpful? Why?
2. In view of the difficulty in understanding verse 12 is it possible to assert dogmatically that though the Holy Spirit may have given a teaching gift to some Christians, if they happen to be female they cannot use it? Give reasons for your answer.
3. Do you think that there is one rule for women in the church and another for women in politics, business and public life generally? Why? Why not? For instance is it acceptable to

have a queen or woman prime minister but not a female Archbishop of Canterbury?

Interpreting verse 12

The interpretation of this verse is more difficult than appears from first sight of our English translation. Here are several possible ways of understanding it.

1. Is Paul prohibiting all women everywhere from ever teaching men in churches? This is the way some traditionalists continue to understand it, but it ignores the declaration in Acts 2:17–21 that in the new apostolic age both men and women will prophesy and that the Spirit will be poured out on both genders. Luke underscores this in recording the prophesying of Mary, Elizabeth and Anna at the start of his two-volume work. It also ignores the obvious fact of teaching gifts given to women by the Holy Spirit both in the overseas mission field and here at home (whenever those gifts are recognized and used). One writer expresses the problem like this: 'In no other verse of Scripture is it stated that women are not to be in authority over men. It is precarious indeed to deny that women should ever be in a position of authority over men based on this disputed meaning of the only occurrence of this word anywhere in the Bible.' (Philip Payne, *Trinity Journal*, 1981)

2. Is Paul prohibiting women from giving false teaching only in Ephesus? That is, it was a local stopgap measure banning women from teaching this particular error at this particular time and place and not 'hard on women' as some might think: after all, two men have just been excommunicated. Silencing these women who are teaching error is a milder, gentler way of dealing with the issue. But can we be right regarding some biblical statements as having only limited and local application?

Expressions like 'Christ Jesus came into the world to save sinners' are always and everywhere true. Other statements are of limited application like 'bring the cloak that I left ... at Troas' (2 Timothy 4:13). None of us thinks that this means we must make pilgrimages to Troas to fetch cloaks. But this verse about women false teachers is a classic example of an intermediate position between these two extremes. Another is found in 1 Timothy 5:14: specific advice to widows in Ephesus differs from general advice to widows in 1 Corinthians 7:8. Many, however, still feel our English translation sounds like a general prohibition (see '*I do not permit*', p. 63).

3. Is Paul just prohibiting wives from teaching their husbands? Wife and woman are often the same word in Greek (as Ephesians 5:22, 'wives submit to your own husbands'). So if we translate 'I do not permit a *wife* to teach or domineer over her husband', this is a quite different sentiment and no problem. Neither husband nor wife ought to domineer over each other. Advice about prayer and dress, however, are clearly for all women whether married or not, so this seems an improbable solution.

The meaning of *authentein*

But if none of these explanations are fully satisfying, what then? Some scholars find a way out of the impasse by pointing out that Paul uses a very unusual word for 'have authority over', *authentein*. It is so unusual that we cannot be sure this is the right translation and in fact cannot be sure of its meaning at all, and this gives rise to four more possible interpretations.

4. Is Paul not prohibiting all teaching, but only domineering, bossy teaching? This is not a ban on women ever teaching on any subject, but only specifically against domineering teaching. The heart of the problem is deciding the meaning of a verb which only occurs here, that is, once in the whole New Testament. So we have to puzzle out the meaning from its use in

non-biblical writing. Formerly people picked out those uses in secular Greek, which supported the translation they liked. But today the existence of an exciting new computer database has changed all that, making it possible to examine many different usages of a word (see *How computers ... can help*, p. 64).

5. Does the word have some idiomatic local meaning understood by Paul's audience but not by us? This rare word might be shorthand for a whole position, just as words like 'prosperity' or 'shepherding' become a shorthand way of expressing a particular emphasis (or error), implying far more than their literal meaning. Paul uses both 'knowledge' and 'wisdom' that way too.

6. Is Paul prohibiting a particular false teaching – that women are the origin of men? This is argued by Kathy Kroeger, a classical scholar researching myths and similar literature connected with Ephesus (see For Further Reading). Ephesus was supposedly founded by a tribe of female Amazon warriors, who claimed their descent from their mothers and treated men as slaves. The word originally meant 'to be the author, or perpetrator of a crime especially murder' (see *How computers ... can help*, p. 64). After reviewing many possible meanings, Kroeger suggests that we might translate it, 'I do not allow a woman to teach or to proclaim herself the author of man', that is, that women are forbidden to claim the power of origin and to teach that female activity brought man into existence, especially that Eve existed before Adam (see on verse 13 below). Some ancient myths in Ephesus even taught that the Creator God of Genesis was himself created by a supreme female being known as 'Authentia'! This fits the context, condemning myths and genealogies (1:4), and correcting the error of Eve being made before Adam (2:13: see quotes from heretical writings in *Myths in Asia Minor*, p. 69).

7. Is Paul prohibiting cultic fornication? In the book of Proverbs (2:18; 5:5; 7:27) sexual sin leads figuratively to death: here,

mystery cult prostitutes might lure men to spiritual death. Michael Green, choosing the older meaning of this word, 'to perpetrate a crime' (usually murder) writes, 'The background of the word is sex and murder ... Paul is not allowing women in orgiastic Ephesus to slaughter men by leading them into cultic fornication' (*Freed to Serve* (Word, 1983), p. 88). We need to know more of the background but human bones have been found mingled with those of animals in the sacrifice pits of Diana's temple in Ephesus. Human sacrifice to Artemis in Asia Minor is attested well beyond the New Testament period.

Conclusion

If you find all these attempted solutions confusing it just shows how hard it is to be sure that we can translate this verse correctly. How stupid then to be dogmatic when it is so difficult to decide what the verb translated as 'to have authority over' actually means! This being so, can it be right to use it as a big stick to decide the role of women in churches around the world?

 'I do not permit', always, everywhere?

The English translation 'I do not permit' sounds final, implying 'I never permit' (verse 12). But 'I am not permitting' actually lacks the force of being an universal rule for every situation and rather gives Paul's advice for a particular situation. Every time this verb is used in the Greek translation of the Old Testament it refers to specific situations. In the New Testament while it does occur as 'It is not permitted' (1 Corinthians 14:34), nowhere else is it used as 'I do not ...'

How computers today can help us better to translate the Bible

(You can skip this unless you are fascinated by the meaning of words.)

A new computer database can help us understand the way this verb, to have authority over, which is used only once in the New Testament, was used in other old writings. This is the TLG database at the University of California, Irvine, and is now available to computer buffs and libraries on CD-ROM. This contains some 63 million words of ancient Greek from Homer to AD 600.

This database tells us that the word *authentein* and its close relations appear 329 times outside the Bible. From 500–283 BC it always meant 'to commit a crime (usually murder)'.

Christian writers from AD 182 onwards all use the word in the later sense of 'have authority over'. Somewhere in the 500 years between these dates the word changed its meaning. Authors in Paul's time could use the word with either meaning. So which did Paul mean?

The answer is that we still do not know, but there are more Greek words still to be analysed from papyri on a database at Duke University, so that the material we have available is still incomplete. The riddle may be solved some day!

1 Timothy 2:13–15

Three errors of the false teachers

Paul sets the record straight about some myths and superstitions behind the false teachings in Ephesus.

Error 1. Eve existed before Adam

For Adam was formed first, then Eve (verse 13).

At first sight the train of thought here is so obscure that John Calvin wrote 'Still, Paul's argument, that woman is subject, because she was created second, does not seem to be very strong, for John the Baptist went before Christ in time and yet was far inferior to Him'. More, as the Bible tells us that animals were created first, then the human male and last of all, the female, it might be argued that woman is the summit of creation, because she was created last! Paul is more likely to be referring to the false teaching that Eve was Adam's mother before she was his wife. This 'genealogy' (1:4) was based upon a literal understanding of Genesis 3:20, so making Eve into a mother-goddess. Ephesus and Asia Minor were full of goddess cults in those days, and some Christians were easily conned into making room for them in their beliefs. (See *Myths in Asia Minor*, p. 69 for actual quotations from first-century Ephesus.)

Error 2. Eve was the source of knowledge who taught Adam

It was the woman who was deceived (verse 14). Sometimes it is argued that Eve was responsible for the fall because it was she whom the serpent deceived (and she went ahead and made the decision without consulting her partner, which she should have done). But Paul blames Adam in Romans 5:12–14 and does not even mention Eve there. The woman may have been deceived, but Adam was not and he deliberately and knowingly chose to sin in disobeying God. It took Satan to deceive Eve, but only a mere woman to deceive Adam!

Others see this as an argument about women's incapacity to teach based upon so-called 'creation ordinances' (a man-made idea: the expression is never found in the Bible!). What is the point of the comment? Can it possibly mean that Paul believes all women to be gullible and more easily deceived than men? Scarcely. Where women are concerned, men are far more gullible! Timothy himself was taught by two women; Priscilla instructed Apollos; Paul speaks of men and women who can teach others (2 Timothy 2:2); while older women can teach younger women (Titus 2:3). We know that some women are much more discerning than some men. We should shun foolish gender stereotypes which belittle men and women whom God has created.

Again it seems possible, however, that the correct answer may lie in the Ephesian myths about Adam and Eve (see p. 70); that Eve taught Adam 'wisdom'. Paul utterly rejects this error. Adam was not deceived and, far from the woman being the source of Adam's knowledge, she was 'totally deceived'. In these two verses, then, Paul refutes two tenets of false teaching in Ephesus. It is these 'myths and genealogies' which lie behind verses 13 and 14, and it is the teaching of these false doctrines by a particular woman (or women) which Paul forbids (verse 12).

Error 3. Help in childbearing came from a mother goddess

What does Paul mean by *saved through childbearing* (verse 15)? Is this a new way to heaven, not open to men? Or does it mean that Christian women who *continue in faith* will be immune to pain or death in childbirth? Neither of these answers will do. The original Greek was 'the childbearing' and some translations (for example, the Amplified Bible) interpret it as referring to the birth of *the* child, Jesus. This also seems unlikely.

Some traditionalists maintain that it means that women who do not usurp man's role as teacher, but stick to childbearing and home keeping, as wives and mothers, will know the blessing of God. This would then tie in with Paul's words in 5:14, *I counsel younger widows to marry, to have children.*

Yet others point out that some rabbis taught that humans were more open to temptation at some times than others. Childbirth was a time of peril for young mothers. At the time of childbirth Satan becomes the accuser of the mother. This promise to mothers who *continue in faith, love and holiness with propriety* means they will be *kept safe* through this time of childbearing.

My missionary experience teaches me, however, that in certain areas of life, especially sickness, childbirth and death, old folk rites and beliefs persist even in the church. When people fall sick they return to folk medicine. When babies are due, and perhaps especially if an unconverted mother or mother-in-law is present, the pressure to follow the old ways can be very strong. We know that in Ephesus Diana was closely connected with childbearing rituals. Because she was identified with Cybele, Diana became a gynaecological goddess in Ephesus! Artemis (Diana) was the goddess of birth and as a newborn baby is actually said to have assisted her own mother in the birth of her twin brother, Apollo!

Christian women, then, need to see that safety in childbirth is not to be achieved through the pagan custom of invoking the help of Artemis, but by 'continuing in faith' in the One true God. They will be kept through the stress of bearing children by holding fast to trust in God without reverting to the old folk-superstitions and worship of Artemis. Paul is not opposed to the ministry of women, but to false teaching that is misleading women.

Conclusion

After looking at this somewhat complex passage, it would seem extremely unwise to extract one phrase, *I do not permit a woman to teach*, out of what everyone agrees is a difficult context, and to make that one verse decide the role of women in churches all over the world. Moreover, how could Paul be consistent if he condemned the ministry of women? For elsewhere he calls women his colleagues, members of the same team (Philippians 4:3). In Romans 16 he commends no less than seven women, one after the other: Tryphena, Tryphosa, Persis, Mary (all of whom labour in the Lord), Phoebe, Priscilla and, almost certainly, Junia. Scripture must be consistent with itself and so must the apostle Paul.

Questions

1. Are there situations in our culture in which old folk-beliefs occasionally try to reassert themselves? Take Christmas as an example, and Halloween as another. What is good and/or bad in all this?
2. When you cannot understand what a passage of Scripture means, how do you set about finding out (prayer, commentaries, ministers, friends)? And what if none of them satisfy you?
3. Has Christianity contributed to the emancipation of women? Compare cultures with a Christian tradition with others without it.

Myths in Asia Minor (relevant to verse 13)

Kroeger's research into the pagan climate and Jewish myths in Asia Minor in the first century give us possible insights into Paul's train of thought here. Artemis's predecessor Cybele was known as the Mountain Mother, and over seventy inscriptions honouring her have been found in Ephesus. She was the great Mother Goddess of Asia Minor and when the Greeks arrived, Artemis assumed much of the character and functions of her predecessor. In a similar way in Egypt, Eve was identified with Isis. Jewish people in Ephesus knew the scripture that Eve was the mother of 'all living' (Genesis 3:20) and the myth developed that she pre-existed Adam and was his mother before she was his wife. There is a real problem in dating these references but they give some clue as to the wild ideas floating around at that time.

> For Eve is the first virgin, the one who had no male and yet gave birth. She is the one who acted as physician midwife to herself.
>
> *On the Origin of the World* 113. 33

Or again:

> The spirit-filled woman came to him. She spoke with him, saying 'Arise, Adam'. And when he saw her he said 'You are the one who has given me life. You will be called the mother of the living, because she is my mother, she is the female healer, and the woman and the one who gave birth.'
>
> *The Hypostasis of the Archons* 2, 89, 11–16

These and other references represent Eve as pre-existing Adam.

More myths in Asia Minor (relevant to verse 14)

One story of the time tells how the so-called 'higher powers' trick Adam into believing he was made first:

> Let us bring sleep upon him (Adam) and let us teach him in sleep, as if she came into being from his rib so that the woman may be subject and he may be lord over her.
>
> *(On the Origin of the World* 2.5, 116)

So the 'truth' is exactly the opposite of what Genesis actually says! This twisting of the original could have been written today by someone with a sexist axe to grind.

Paul shows that so far from being the source of all knowledge, and being the teacher of Adam, Eve was totally deceived by the serpent. Among the false myths the view that Eve was a spiritual instructor with superior knowledge was strongly entrenched. Thus Adam is made to say:

> She (Eve) instructed me with an account of knowledge of the eternal god.
>
> *(Apocalypse of Adam)*

Other views include the notion that the serpent made Eve wise, perhaps even having sexual relations with her, and then, in turn, the woman made the man wise. Epiphanius speaks of a Gospel of Eve named after her, because she 'discovered the food of *gnōsis* (divine knowledge) through revelation spoken to her by the snake.'

For a comparison of the concerns regarding women in chapters 2 and 5 see p. 108.

FINDING NEW CHURCH LEADERS

1 Timothy 3

1 Timothy 3:1–7

Qualities to be looked for in overseers (bishops) or elders

**Fifteen pointers to the kind of person
God calls to guide his people.**

The Ephesian church was disappointed with
its leaders. It had had elders for some years
(see Acts 20:27), but some had proved so
unfit they had been put out of the church
(1:20). So Paul gives them a do-it-yourself guide to selecting
leaders. This is not a bland list of what to look for in any good
local church leader ('in case you might need to appoint leaders
some time'), but pointed and loaded: they must take care not to
appoint anyone else who is sexually irresponsible, addicted to
alcohol, quarrelsome, greedy for money or unsound in doctrine.

In verse 1 we meet the second of Paul's 'trustworthy sayings'
(see p. 41) though this one is practical, not theological. Paul may
be endorsing something they have said, or it may have been a
common saying. It is not wrong to want to be a church leader if
the church thinks you fit for it. It is a noble task or literally a
'beautiful work', a worthwhile job. It is all right to set your heart
(the word means to stretch out towards something – the original
Greek of 6:10 uses it of 'eager for money') on leadership, if that
is what God is calling you to, but you should beware of wrong

motives, of wanting to be centre stage. (In times of persecution, people hesitate to become leaders; they are often the first to be arrested!)

The marks of a good leader

What follows is not a 'job description', but a character profile: 'This is the kind of person who is fit to lead.' Some see these virtues as unspiritual but any missionary who has tried to find fit leaders among recent converts in a young church knows that such down to earth things still matter today.

1. *Above reproach* (verse 2). There must be no defect of character or conduct in past or present life which could be used to discredit them. Blameless character is placed first. It is tragic when Christian leaders lose public trust because of moral failure. They lose their ministry, but the church loses credibility. This first statement summarizes all that follows.

2. *Husband of one wife* (verse 2). This could mean an overseer must be married; or ought not to remarry (conflicts with 5:14); or not be a polygamist (some Jews and pagans had second wives or concubines). We take it to mean blameless and faithful in marriage.

3. *Temperate* (verse 2) means 'clearheaded': alcohol addiction is covered in verse 3.

4. *Self-controlled* (verse 2), prudent. Paul often uses this word in the Pastoral letters. It implies total command over one's passions and desires (a Greek virtue, much admired also by Chinese sages and Japanese samurai).

5. *Respectable* (verse 2), well behaved. It relates to the word for 'adorn': inner self-control produces outward dignity, a shining face for all to see.

6. *Hospitable* (verse 2). Literally 'loving foreigners', the opposite of xenophobia, hatred of alien cultures. The travelling stranger in New Testament times was always at risk of being cheated, mugged and robbed. Churches provided respectable 'safe-houses' for believing wayfarers. Overseers must set an example of hospitality.

7. *Able to teach* (as 2 Timothy 2:24). The closest to an 'academic' qualification in the list. Today many assume that college education is essential for ministry. It is useful, of course, but a theology degree does not give a person the charismatic gift of teaching. In New Testament churches some elders were teachers (see 1 Timothy 5:17) so it was a disaster when they taught error in Ephesus.

8. *Not given to much wine* (verse 3), not a slave to drink. This was evidently a huge problem in the early church for both men and women (see, for instance, 1 Corinthians 5:11; 11:21 (at the Lord's table); 1 Peter 4:3). They are not told to be total abstainers (but note Romans 14:21), but must avoid anything that weakens self-control. It is wise for us to err on the side of caution, whether we are driving a car or not.

9. *Not violent* (verse 3). This word, from which we derive 'plectrum', means a giver of blows, a brawler who assaults others. Violence is not unheard of in church assemblies today.

10. *Gentle* (verse 3), patient, forbearing, gracious, readily forgiving like Jesus himself (2 Corinthians 10:1).

11. *Not quarrelsome* (verse 3). The word sounds like the opposite of 'macho' and means inoffensive, peaceable, not aggressive, trigger-happy, looking for a fight (1 Timothy 1:4; 2:8 and 6:4, 5 suggest they had had just such leaders). Jesus says his disciples are to lead by example rather than by throwing their weight around (Matthew 20:25–28; 23:8–12; 1 Peter 5:3).

12. *Not a lover of money* (verse 3), literally 'silver'. For example, see Simon Magus (Acts 8:20). Paul's constant warnings against greed (3:8; 6:5, 9, 10) show that the false teachers were greedy for money. Next to sexual failure, greed for money is the greatest cause for scandal among church leaders around the world. We should pray for one another accordingly.

13. *He must manage his own family well* (verse 4) or 'keep his children in control with unruffled dignity'. A chaotic home life suggests unfitness for office. Paul does not seem to envisage the idea of a celibate priesthood. *Manage* means 'preside over' (translated as 'govern' in Romans 12:8; and 'over you' in 1 Thessalonians 5:12). See *Teenage Traumas*, p. 77.

14. *Not a recent convert* (verse 6), literally not a new plant (see 1 Corinthians 3:6). Over-rapid promotion makes people elated and inflated: *the same judgment as the devil* points to Lucifer's sin of pride (referred to in Isaiah 14:12). Puffed up leaders deserve the same fate as the devil. Paul is referring here to God's judgment of Satan for the devil does not judge us.

15. *He must also have a good reputation* (verse 7) among Jews and pagans alike. The little man with a big Bible, with little status in society at large, may try to compensate by trying to be a big noise in the church. Paul does not mean that people who are of high rank in society are automatically fitted for church leadership. But church leaders should have made some impact on the world outside, so that non-Christians respect them for their integrity and achievements. If the devil, who makes war on the saints, can disgrace and discredit church leaders, his trap succeeds. Such leaders are vulnerable as the Enemy's prime targets.

Questions

1. Make your own list of qualities you would look for in church officers today and compare them with those given by the apostle. Give reasons for any differences.
2. If you aspire to 'a noble task' of church leadership, how far do you fit these requirements? What changes might you need to make in your own life?
3. How should we react when church leaders are publicly exposed for scandalous behaviour?

Overseers, bishops and elders

'Overseer' was a common title for superintendents in Gentile societies. The word occurs five times in the New Testament (here; Acts 20:28 of this same church; Philippians 1:1; Titus 1:7; 1 Peter 2:25 of the Lord Jesus Christ). Comparing Acts 20:17 with 20:28 and Titus 1:5 with 1:7 we see that in both passages overseer and elder are different titles for the same people. 'Elder' points to their age and 'overseer' to what they do. While a modern ordained 'bishop' in, for example, the Anglican or Roman Catholic churches supervises many congregations, the New Testament uses the word for one among several leaders within one local church. These will have been 'lay' leaders, as is usually the case of 'elders' in free church traditions today. The New Testament speaks of elders in the plural (Acts 14:23; 20:17; Titus 1:5), so although this passage uses the singular form 'the overseer', it has a plural meaning, just as when we speak of 'a committee member' it implies one of a wider group (compare 'the widow' (5:4, 5) or 'a student' (Luke 6:40)).

Men and women as elders?

In these verses the NIV inserts 'he' or 'his' eleven times though the original Greek has no male personal pronouns here. Grammatically the *anyone* of verse 1 must refer to persons of either sex so this passage does not exclude women from being elders. Most elders may have been men and so Paul expects them to be the husband of one wife (verse 2). The same expression is used of deacons (verse 12) yet we know that Phoebe was a female deacon and 'patroness' of the Cenchrean church (Romans 16:1–2). This phrase does not exclude from office those who may be childless, unmarried or not a man at all. But all must be blameless in sexual matters.

Teenage traumas

Paul expects church officers to manage their families well (verse 4). Ironically it often seems to happen that children brought up more strictly than their friends react more violently against parental control, especially when they reach teenage years. Many loving and prayerful parents feel guilty if their teenagers become wilful, feeling it reflects badly on them, their church and the Lord. Some, therefore, feel they should not accept appointment or even resign from office if their children fail to 'come up to scratch' or have not yet come to a personal faith. It seems to me that while a person's household management may be a helpful rule of thumb when first appointing elders, we should not regard subsequent rebellion of growing children as a cause of disqualification. We certainly need to pray for the children of our church leaders.

1 Timothy 3:8–13

Qualities to be looked for in male and female deacons

Paul now turns to deacons. Again he is more concerned with character than job descriptions.

Having considered overseers, Paul turns to deacons, 'likewise' (indicating a parallel class). The word 'deacon' is used more generally of 'servants', but five times it refers  to an office: Phoebe, Romans 16:1; Philippians 1:1 and verses 8, 10, 12 here. 'The Seven' (Acts 6) are never called deacons in the text, though they have often been identified as such. It is tempting to identify the gift of overseers with 'gifts of administration', and of deacons as 'those able to help others' (1 Corinthians 12:28) and contributing to the needs of others (Romans 12:8). It seems that deacons do not need a teaching gift. The acceptable character profile follows a similar pattern to that of elders, but is shorter.

- They are to be *worthy of respect* (verse 8), dignified or serious, like Christians generally (2:2) and elders in particular (3:4).

- *sincere* (verse 8), not double-tongued (AV), that is, saying one thing to please one and the opposite to please another.

▶ *not indulging in much wine* (verse 8), that is, not addicted.

▶ *not pursuing dishonest gain* (verse 8). If these people had charge of the funds, they must be reliable. (1 Timothy 6:5, 9, 10 suggests that their predecessors in office had failed at this point, so the comment is loaded.)

▶ *They must keep hold of the deep truths of the faith* (verse 9) for while treasurers, stewards and givers of notices may not be called to teach others, they need to know what they believe and why.

▶ *They must first be tested* (verse 10). 'Test' means to approve after careful screening as to conduct, character and fitness. If the Ephesians had been more careful in appointing leaders in the first place, they might have avoided the false teaching now threatening their existence. Churches today still need to be vigilant and careful.

Women deacons?

In the original Greek verse 11 begins 'likewise women'. Are these deacons' wives (NIV) or are they female deacons (NIV footnote)? The second seems more correct because:

▶ Use of 'likewise' puts them in a parallel class with deacons (verse 8) and the overseers.

▶ The text says *women* and does not use the possessive pronoun 'their women' (the same Greek word translates as both woman and wife).

▶ If deacons' wives were meant we could have expected mention of the overseers' wives following verse 7.

▶ The word 'deacon' does not have a feminine form in the Bible and is used here like an adjective, 'deacons who are women'.

▶ Women are mentioned elsewhere in this role: Phoebe is specifically called 'deacon'; also Mary, Persis, Tryphena and Tryphosa (Romans 16); and Euodia and Syntyche (Philippians 4:2), whom Paul calls colleagues and members of the same team.

This evidence suggests that the New Testament knew a parallel order of women deacons. At times in church history they have been called 'Bible women', as in China still. They are to be *worthy of respect* (verse 11) like the men; not malicious talkers, a word meaning 'devil' in the singular form and 'slanderers' in the plural; *temperate*, that is, clearheaded. (When Bishop J. C. Ryle described what he was looking for in a wife he said, 'A Christian, a lady and not a fool!') Finally they are to be trustworthy in everything. Reliability is a human virtue supremely demonstrated by Christian women.

Good service produces good results!

The return to *deacon* (verse 12) seems to confirm the inclusion of women in this context as being deacons. The male married deacons must have the same standing as husbands and fathers as the elders (see verses 2–5). It is not that they *must* be married with children but that they *may* be, and unmarried men and women are not excluded. There is a majority of women in most British churches today: if a church has a plural leadership (as biblically it should), it seems most unwise not to include some women, not only to represent the many women in the church, but because of the contribution they can make in their own right.

Those who have served well gain an excellent standing (verse 13). *Standing* is a word found only here in the New Testament and it means 'step' or 'foundation' and so a degree of rank. It need not mean automatic promotion to the rank of overseer in due course. It is not clear why doing one's job well gives standing and assurance. Perhaps when we affirm church leaders for doing their job well this makes them more confident in continuing their tasks. Faith, tested by service in the real world of needy people, will grow and become more secure.

Questions

1. In what ways has your Christian service helped to strengthen your own faith?
2. Compare these lists with Titus 1:5–9. Are the purposes of these two lists the same or different. If so, how?
3. How does your church give women opportunity to serve and lead? Should they have more/fewer? Why? What could be done to improve the situation along the lines of these verses?

1 Timothy 3:14–16

Paul's reason for writing

Paul sends the letter in case he is delayed. He concludes this section with a burst of praise.

The train of thought in verse 16 is not easy to follow. Although Paul expected to revisit Ephesus he covers the possibility of being delayed by sending this letter. He was in fact rearrested and prevented from returning, but the Ephesian church will know how they ought to conduct themselves in God's household: this was the purpose of the letter.

Paul describes the church of the living God as *the pillar and foundation of the truth* (verse 15). Asia Minor is strewn with pillars, but here Paul is probably recalling the pillars of the great temple of Diana at Ephesus. It was three times larger than the Parthenon in Athens, which was dedicated to the virgin goddess of wisdom, Athene. The Ephesus temple is a ruin today, but the pillars from it may still be seen in St Sophia in Istanbul (the Emperor Justinian had them brought on barges from Ephesus for his great basilica there).

To the Ephesians Paul had written 'In him (that is, Christ) the whole building is joined together and rises to become a holy temple in the Lord' (2:21). Paul perhaps saw each new congregation he planted as one more pillar or buttress built into the incomplete temple of the universal church. Each new congregation is fresh evidence of the power of God. Every new church planted strengthens the evidence for the truth. This verse provides a unique illustration relating each local church to other congregations within the whole great temple of the total world church. *The mystery of godliness is great* (verse 16) may have been a deliberate parody of 'Great is Artemis of the Ephesians' (Acts 19:28, 34).

Practical instructions lead into praising God

The list of virtues looked for in church officers is followed by a 'doxology', a spontaneous burst of praise. This one reads like poetry, an excerpt from a hymn about the Lord Jesus. Paul does not separate church business from worship, as some of our committees tend to do. The hymn can be seen as three pairs of couplets – flesh and spirit, angels and nations, world and glory (i.e., earth and heaven).

- *He appeared in a body.* The incarnation of the Lord Jesus, who 'made his dwelling among us' (John 1:14).

- *Was vindicated by the Spirit*, perhaps referring to the Holy Spirit descending on him like a dove at his baptism (Matthew 3:16), anointing him as the Christ or Messiah,

82

when his Father affirmed, 'This is my Son, whom I love; with him I am well pleased' (Matthew 3:16).

▶ *Was seen by angels.* Angels again and again appear in Jesus' life, for they long to investigate the meaning of the gospel (1 Peter 1:12). His birth is announced by one angel (Luke 1:26–38); heralded by another, accompanied by their choir (Luke 2:9–15). Angels served him after his temptation (Mark 1:13), strengthened him in Gethsemane (Luke 22:43), stood by in squadrons to rescue him if he called them (Matthew 26:53), appeared at his resurrection (John 20:12) and after his ascension (Acts 1:10). They crowd around him (John 1:51) and will escort him back when he returns (Matthew 16:27).

▶ *Preached among the nations.* If angels were closest to God, the Gentile nations were considered to be 'afar off': but Christ's death was to bring them near (Ephesians 2:13). Paul was their herald and he may have quoted this hymn as a deliberate counter to exclusivist Jewish false teaching (see 1 Timothy 2:1, 4, 5).

▶ *Believed on in the world.* In the previous couplet we moved from angels in heaven to nations on earth. This couplet reverses the order and now we move from believers in the world to glory in heaven. Not only in Jerusalem and in Judaea, but to the ends of the earth Jesus is proclaimed and believed on.

▶ *Taken up in glory* may refer to the Shekinah glory (the rabbis used the word to mean the radiance of God's real presence) seen by Ezekiel, and by the apostles at Jesus' trans-figuration (Matthew 17:1–8), but here it refers to Jesus' ascension to heaven. The list of leadership qualifications lead to this burst of heavenly praise: this is what we have local church leaders for, to help fulfil the ministry of Jesus in building his church.

83

Questions

1. What local or recent illustrations could you use to explain your church as the *pillar and foundation of the truth*?
2. Rewrite this ancient hymn (verse 16) in your own words, and use it in worship.
3. Read all the references to angels given above. Do we give them too little prominence today? How much do you expect them to influence us?

4

FALSE TEACHING REFUTED

1 Timothy 4

1 Timothy 4:1–5

False teaching refuted by sound teaching

**When God gives us good things to enjoy
it is very wrong to forbid people to enjoy them.**

Paul turns first to the nature of the false
teaching which Timothy has been commanded to stop (verses 1–5); and second, to
the nature of Timothy's ministry if he is to
succeed in stopping it (verses 6–16). At first sight it seems as if
the subject changes from replacing church leaders to false
teaching, but there are no chapter breaks in the original text and
the connecting word 'however' is omitted by the NIV. The train
of thought may be: 'The church is the pillar and foundation of
truth, however the Spirit has warned us of *error*. There is no
point in being carried away in worship (3:16) if you allow false
teaching to flourish.' Paul wants Timothy (and us) to grasp
where the false teaching comes from, the kind of people who are
spreading it and how to combat it by sound biblical teaching.

False teaching is not unexpected. The Holy Spirit forewarned
us clearly (verse 1). Paul had certainly warned the Ephesian
leaders about it (Acts 20:29), echoing the teaching of Jesus
(Matthew 7:15). *Later times* means the present, not necessarily
the same as 'the Last Days' when the Second Coming is

imminent (2 Timothy 3:1). Some respected members of God's household (3:15), that is, our churches, will abandon the faith and fall away from basic Christian truth (see Matthew 24:12). We must do all we can to avoid this tragedy, but it should not surprise or disillusion us when it happens.

The source of the false teaching is demonic (verse 1). The deception is powerful because it is not merely human in origin: Satan can disguise himself as an angel of light (2 Corinthians 2:11; 11:14). Teachers may sincerely believe they are being faithful to truth, while being deceived into falsehood. Compare the 'lying spirit' in the story of Micaiah, son of Imlah (1 Kings 22:19–23). That such demonic attack was widespread in Asia Minor is clear from the Letters to Smyrna, Pergamum, Thyatira and Philadelphia (Revelation 2:9, 13, 24; 3:9).

The human agents know full well what they are doing, for they are play-acting hypocrites (verse 2), pretending to be super-spiritual when they are no such thing. Their *consciences have been seared with a hot iron*. Hippocrates, a Greek authority on medicine, used these words of cauterizing apparatus. It suggests that these people were numb to truth (Ephesians 4:19), or perhaps branded by a Satanic branding iron, marking his ownership. God has agents committed to his service, but sadly Satan also has tools committed to his (compare John 8:44).

God's good gifts denied

Two specific examples of false teaching show how wrong these deceived teachers could be (verse 3).

1. Forbidding marriage

It appears that such teaching was widespread (see 1 Corinthians 7:1; Hebrews 13:4). The fact that Paul will shortly advise young widows to remarry (1 Timothy 5:14) shows it was a problem in Ephesus too. The Greeks believed that matter is evil, that our bodies and therefore sex is unclean, so it is better to be virgin than to marry. Perhaps Buddhist dogma about destroying desire had travelled westwards along trade routes from Persia. The Roman Catholic Church officially still insists on celibate clergy which seems to perpetuate the same error that it is better to be a virgin than to marry. Sir Thomas More was angry with Martin Luther for marrying his Katharine. This later error may have been a reaction against pagan promiscuity and license, but it fails to grasp that God the Creator is good; that he made us male and female; he invented our sexuality, which, when expressed within marriage must be a good thing. Proverbs 5:15–19 gives a picture of uninhibited God-given joy in marriage.

2. Abstaining from certain foods

This error also seems widespread (see 1 Corinthians 10:23–33; Romans 14:1–23 and Colossians 2:16, 21). It may have come from the self-styled teachers of the Jewish Law (1:7). Christians have been liberated from the bondage of rules and regulations. God means us to receive his gifts with thanksgiving and not reject them by sliding back into narrow legalism and superstition.

Error countered by positive teaching

For everything God created is good (verse 4). 'Everything' is emphasized. 'Good' means beautiful to look at. We are reminded of the sevenfold 'God saw that it was good' from Genesis 1. The whole earth is full of God's glory (Isaiah 6:3), because the earth is his and all that is in it (Psalm 24:1). It belongs to God and is good. In the past monastics have tended to refuse to enjoy the world's gifts; other Christians to transform and enjoy God's lavish gifts.

Nothing is to be rejected or treated as taboo. They knew the truth (verse 3) that Christ had declared all food clean (Mark 7:19) and had taught Peter this in a vision (Acts 10:15).

Received with thanksgiving refers to giving thanks before meals (see, for example, Romans 14:6; 1 Corinthians 10:30) and the example of Jesus (Mark 6:41; 8:6; 14:22; Luke 24:30). 'Saying Grace' must be more than a traditional formality giving permission to eat, but a response from the heart, 'Lord, you made this so good and we accept it with gladness' (see Acts 2:46).

Consecrated by the Word of God and prayer (verse 5). It is not that prayer cleanses what was previously unclean, but that the word of God shows us that it is already clean and good. Grace properly prayed sets food in its proper perspective (see Psalm 104:14–15, 27–28).

Questions

1. How are we to enjoy God's good creation? Make a list of activities under the heading 'enjoying God's goods'. Discuss how you can do more enjoying!
2. What do these verses say to us about the importance of 'giving thanks' at meals? Is it out of place in modern society?
3. How far should the church react to the words of secular society by changing its stance (e.g. on homosexuality or couples living together before marriage) and how far should it be inflexible? If inflexible, where should the rules come from?

False teaching in Ephesus, Corinth and Colosse

We often talk as though New Testament cities were utterly isolated from each other, and their 'heresies' quite distinct. But false teachers can travel as fast as true apostles, and the following table show that there are common features in all these places. Letters to the Seven Churches of Asia Minor (Revelation 2–3) show similar parallels.

False teaching	Ephesus	Corinth	Colosse	Asia Minor
Legalism	1 Timothy 1:7–9		Colossians 2:16, 21	
Asceticism	1 Timothy 4:3	1 Corinthians 7:1–7	Colossians 2:16–23	
Speculations	1 Timothy 1:4			
Resurrection	2 Timothy 2:18	1 Corinthians 15:12		
'Knowledge'	1 Timothy 6:20	1 Corinthians 8:1–2	Colossians 2:3–8	
Exclusivism	1 Timothy 2:4–6	1 Corinthians 1:12	Colossians 1:28	
Satanism	1 Timothy 5:15	1 Corinthians 10:20		Revelation 2: 9, 13, 24
Sexual sin	2 Timothy 3:6	1 Corinthians 6:9		Revelation 2: 14, 20

1 Timothy 4:6–16

The marks of a true teacher

Timothy is to be as great a contrast as possible with those who have been teaching error in Ephesus.

The rest of the chapter turns from the correction of errors being taught by others to the problems Timothy faces in putting into practice the positive teaching of truth and the negative refuting of error. Paul uses four illustrations of attitudes to be adopted by a Christian worker.

Nourishing children

Paul uses a picture of childrearing, *brought up* (verse 6), to illustrate the importance of Timothy continuing to nourish himself *in the truths of the faith and the good teaching* with which he has familiarized himself. The minister can only feed others if he has first nourished himself. This involved, and still involves, regular, daily feeding on the Word of God (for Paul and Timothy the Old Testament) which is where good teaching comes from. So keep well clear of *godless myths and old wives' tales* (verse 7) that is, bad teaching. Naive Christians then and now are easily conned into believing new, exciting, superspiritual ideas floated by popular gurus. All teaching must be tested and weighed against Scripture and distortions rejected. The positive response to error is a wholesome diet of good theology. *Point these things out to the brothers* (verse 6), namely, the basic truths about God as the good Creator. The teacher thus nourished, can then share these health-giving truths with others.

Physical training

The Greeks were enthusiasts for physical training and athletics – they started the Olympic Games. The Greek word for school was 'gymnasium'. Paul applies this picture of athletic training to spiritual fitness: train yourself to be godly. Like an athlete, Timothy should keep in rigorous spiritual shape! Gymnasts train hard for hours each day, practising over and over until they are perfect. So Christian workers should apply themselves to work at their faith and service. Paul may be contrasting the ascetic denial of false teachers over sex and food, with genuine healthy fitness when he says that physical training is of some value (verse 8), but godliness is of infinitely greater value. Paul echoes Jesus' words about the present life and the life to come (Luke 18:30). Have Christians overreacted against 'pie in the sky when we die' and 'posthumous benefits' preaching? We do not think and teach enough about our glorious destiny in heaven. For this we labour and strive (verse 10), wrestling in the sports arena, which is evidence that we have put our hope in the living God, not a single act of trust, but a continuous settled attitude of heart.

Saviour of all men ('all people' of course) again refutes Jewish exclusivism, as in 2:4–6, for God is the Saviour of all. Jesus gave

91

his life a ransom for all: the gospel is offered universally to all, but not all respond or see the need to be ransomed.

How old was Timothy at this point? We do not know, but young (verse 12) does not mean a teenager, but anyone young enough for military service, i.e., under forty years of age. Some Asian communities respect age so much that all their leaders are at least fifty. Older people perhaps looked down on Timothy because of his inexperience. To overcome criticism, he must excel and set an example in those areas in which younger people are expected to fail, *in speech, in life, in love, in faith and in purity* – a daunting list. But merely exhorting Christians to virtue achieves little unless church leaders give them superb models to follow. When we actually see such an example of evangelizing, preaching or praying, we want to follow and imitate it.

Addiction to teaching

Devote yourself (verse 13) means 'be addicted to' (the same Greek word is used in 1:4 and 3:8). Timothy is to be addicted to reading, preaching and teaching as others are addicted to wine or fables. Paul has a deep sense of being compelled by God (1 Corinthians 9:16), but though Christians should be hardworking, they are not to be 'workaholics'. Such obsessive people fail to be equally fanatical about other God-given responsibilities like loving their wives and children and fulfilling other relationships (see 1 Corinthians 7:32–35). The opposite tendency is laziness, failure to addict oneself to thorough preparation, neglecting both God's calling and God's gifts. The spiritual gift which Timothy was not to neglect (verse 14) was teaching (verses 11, 13, 16). In 2 Timothy 1:6 Paul writes 'fan into flame the gift of God, which is in you through the laying on of my hands'. Both verses may refer to Timothy's commissioning. It is a mistake to think that because God has given us a spiritual gift, we do not need to work to cultivate and develop it.

Progress in study

Be diligent in these matters; give yourself wholly to them, so that everyone may see your progress (verse 15). The original Greek contrasts two forms of the same verb, one negative, 'Do not neglect' (verse 14) and one positive, 'Be diligent' (verse 15). We might say 'Don't disuse, but use'; or, 'Don't lay it down, but take it up'. *Progress* means to 'cut in front', and is used of armies advancing or ships cutting through water, but the word was also used by the Stoics to picture novices advancing in philosophy. This gives us the fourth illustration, progress in study. We are not to remain stationary as Christians, but to keep on making progress: and so much so that others can see that progress. In these days of adult education, we are not limited to the progress we made in teenage education. We can always apply ou. .lves to further study: there are extension courses, distance learning courses and many ways of upgrading ourselves.

These illustrations pile up responsibility on the teacher: go on being nourished like a growing youth; practise like an athlete; be addicted to teaching and make progress like a student. Though Timothy has been given a spiritual gift this does not mean that he has no duty to develop it, cultivate it, and make progress in using it. The plain force of verses 14–16 is that possessing a spiritual gift is not enough, for it can be neglected: it must be worked at. You may be given a book as a gift at Christmas and never read it, or a music album and never play it! You may have a tap and never turn it on. Or even a brain and never use it!

To sum up, Timothy's lifestyle of example (verse 12) and his practise of teaching (verse 13) demands constant hard work. You will save yourself and those who both 'hear' your teaching and 'see' your example. Paul now moves on to the way Timothy must relate to various groups in the church.

Questions

---

1. Is physical fitness (or appearance) more important to you than godliness? Does it play too great a role or too small? What should you do to get the balance right?
2. What do you think churches should do to encourage the ministry of young people like Timothy? How is your church managing in this area?
3. Compare 4:13 with 1 Corinthians 14:26–33. Are these conflicting patterns of worship? How would you reconcile them? See *Christian worship in the early church* below.

Christian worship in the early church

Verse 13 describes public worship as involving three activities: *public reading, preaching and teaching* (in the original Greek all three nouns were preceded by the definite article 'the'). The synagogue custom was to follow public reading of the Law and the prophets by an exposition (explanation) of them. Thus in Pisidian Antioch the elders asked Paul and Barnabas if they had a 'word of encouragement' (Acts 13:15), translated here in verse 13 as *preaching* (NIV). It is the same spiritual gift translated as 'encouragement' in Romans 12:8. It does not mean cheering people up so much as exhorting them from Scripture. It is what Jesus did in the Nazareth synagogue (Luke 4:17–22). If this 'exposition' focused on the Scriptures just read, then the third component *the teaching* would seem to mean instruction from the whole wealth of biblical truth. This is the model followed by the early church. Reading and expounding of Scripture took central place. God's words to us should come before our songs to God. Today the overhead projector seems to have usurped the place formerly held by lectern and pulpit. Churches have become centred upon human beings instead of upon God.

How and when are spiritual gifts given?

Timothy possessed the gift of teaching, received through Paul laying hands on him. Is this how gifts are always given? The Bible gives us three ways.

1. By divine providence at birth

Jeremiah is told that God knew him and formed him in his mother's womb (Jeremiah 1:5). Paul says God 'set me apart from birth' (Galatians 1:15). His natural gifts of leadership and initiative are evident before his conversion. God our Creator is the same God as God our Redeemer. He was not taken by surprise by our conversion! Those natural gifts of being a competent organizer or a clear speaker are sanctified by the Holy Spirit as the spiritual gifts of administration and teaching. Natural gifts are not the same as spiritual gifts, but they are not totally unrelated to them either, because God is the giver of both.

2. By divine sovereignty at conversion

Paul's own conversion experience gives us a model here (Acts 9:15, 20; 22:15; 26:16; 1 Timothy 2:7). God appointed him at that time to be a herald, apostle and teacher. The Bible teaches us that all Christians are members of the body with God-determined and God-given functions to perform (1 Corinthians 12:6, 7, 11, 18). That begins from conversion.

3. By divine provision in the church

Some of us dislike the notion that a rite like laying-on of hands might be used by God, as though performing this ceremony automatically bestows spiritual gifts. However, 1 Timothy 4:14 and 2 Timothy 1:6 says that God does use this way. Moses laid hands on Joshua (Numbers 27:18–23; Deuteronomy 34:9). The early church laid hands on the Seven, and in appointing Barnabas and Saul as missionary apostles (Acts 6:6; 13:3). It seems proper that the Sovereign Giver should use the church as a means of transmitting his grace to that church.

This raises the further question whether it is proper for individuals to 'seek gifts' for themselves (1 Corinthians 12:31 'eagerly desire the greatest gifts'). If Paul teaches that each of us should accept our role as hands, feet, ears or mouths, it contradicts what he is aiming at if we all want to be hands or mouths! What we are to seek is the more excellent way of love – appreciating the differing gifts given to each one by the Lord.

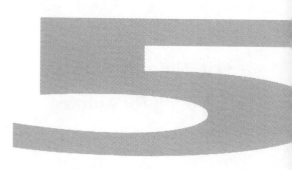

CARING FOR
PEOPLE

1 Timothy 5

1 Timothy 5:1–10

Caring for widows

Paul turns now to deserving widows and their need to be supported by the church. In passing, we meet hints about early church social life and pastoral problems.

First, Paul advises Timothy how to relate generally to older and younger people of both genders. *Do not rebuke an older man harshly* means do not 'rough him up', a verb related to 'striker' (3:3). Even if he has embraced false teaching, a severe reprimand from a younger man would 'take away his face' and destroy his dignity; so exhort him as if he were your father, that is, with respect (see verse 19). Treat younger men as brothers. We are all now related through Christ (see Mark 3:31–35) and should love one another because we are now all fellow members of God's family. In a dead church people relate formally: in a live church people really bond with each other.

Older women as mothers (verse 2: see Romans 16:13 where Rufus' mother has been a mother to Paul). The younger generation, to which Timothy still belongs, must not regard the older generation as 'wrinklies' who are 'past it' but give them respect and warm affection. So treat *younger women as sisters*, with absolute purity. There are temptations for ministers (of either sex) to get emotionally involved with church members.

J. B. Phillips translated this neatly 'as sisters and nothing more'. The mutual bonding within a church provides emotional support and is a witness to the unchurched.

Widows who are in real need (verses 3–5, 7–8)

Godly widows of long standing, who deserve church support, should be treated differently from some 'younger widows' who are causing trouble in Ephesus. Paul deals with deserving cases first, and then the undeserving ones. *Give proper recognition* is translated as 'honour' in older versions and means support financially, pay a stipend, as in the Fifth Commandment, 'Honour your father and mother' (Exodus 20:12), or paying teaching elders 'double honour' (5:17).

Really in need rules out women who still have a family to support them (verse 4). Such relatives cannot shift the burden on to the church. Jesus said that evading caring for parents was breaking God's command (Mark 7:9–13), even if they offered a 'spiritual' reason for it. The point of the Fifth commandment is that your days will be 'long in the land' because your children will support you, having seen the way you cared for your own parents. Your parents cared for you when you were weak and helpless: now you must care for parents and grandparents (the NIV translates a rare word for 'ancestors' only found here and 2 Timothy 1:3). We can assure Chinese friends the Bible does teach care for older members of our families. Those who fail to support their relations are *worse than an unbeliever*. In the ancient world, as in the Third World still, there was no state pension or welfare. It may be less exciting to read to a blind grandmother than to address a youth rally, but which is more pleasing to God, who commands us to meet our parents' needs? God's order is intended to bless all of us.

Widows had a reputation for prayer. Verse 5 includes literally 'the prayers', implying regular church prayer meetings perhaps modelled on the hours of prayer in the temple. The widow asks God for help (see the parable about prayer concerning the widow who went on asking in Luke 18:1–8). The best example of widows praying is Anna who never left the temple but worshipped day and night, fasting and praying (Luke 2:37). In later church history there were religious orders of widows who were committed to spend their time in prayer.

Who deserves to be put on the list? (verses 9–10)

To be *put on the list* was to be enrolled, a word used of soldiers in Greek. The church supported widows from the beginning (see Acts 6:1) but had to be careful and selective. Paul lists here the qualifications necessary for being included.

- *Over sixty*, the age at which one becomes a 'senior citizen' in the west (see Leviticus 27:7) and after which remarriage is less common.

- *Faithful to her husband* probably means 'has had but one husband' (NIV footnote), for if she had remarried she would still have a husband to support her.

- *Well known for her good deeds*. Examples of these include:

- *Bringing up children* – these were probably church orphans, for if they were her own they should be caring for her.

- *Hospitality* – caring for church guests (see Hebrews 13:2).

- *Washing the feet of the saints* – a menial task (1 Samuel 25:41) but an act of humble service commended by the Lord Jesus (John 13:14), who fulfilled the servant's role.

- *Helping those in trouble* suggests a church social programme in which widows played an important role. The 'order of widows' was more like a band of paid church workers than recipients of charity.

- *She should help them* (16); this is not repeating the instructions of verses 4, 8. It suggests that the household of a wealthy female church member (single, married or widowed) should include other widows: let her take care of them and not burden the church. Misunderstanding would arise if a man took care of them, but not if a wealthy woman supported other women.

Questions

1. Make a (private) list of six or so people in your church whom you do not like or know least. How can you show some practical care for them as members of Christ's family?
2. What reasons can you suggest for not having elderly relatives living with in you in the light of this passage?
3. What are the church's priorities? Is it more important for churches to nurture the young or to care for the old?

1 Timothy 5:6, 11–16

Merry widows

Some younger widows had become involved in false teaching so Timothy and the Ephesian church needed guidance in disciplining them.

Living for pleasure (verse 6) does not mean enjoying life, of which Paul approves (4:4–5; 6:17) but sumptuous, self-indulgent living. This rare word, used also in Ezekiel 16:48, describes the 'careless ease' of Sodom, personalized here as female. In James 5:5 it is used of rich people leading a 'life of wanton pleasure'. The sacrificial giving of church members must not be wasted in propping up a luxurious lifestyle, which allowed some women to dress lavishly (2:9). You cannot include all widows on the list without looking at their reputation and lifestyle. *Open to blame* (verse 7) implies that some have not been above reproach or criticism.

What about younger widows who are still full of energy and marriageable? Professor Howard Marshall, in his lectures, calls them 'The Merry Widows'. After the first flush of grief and loss, when it seems they took a vow never to marry again, they may want to change their minds. Paul, at first seems to disapprove of this, suggesting the prompting of their natural passions may overcome their dedication to Christ (verse 11) and that they will have broken their first pledge (verse 12). In view of his condemnation of those who forbid people to marry, however (4:3), he does not think remarriage a wrong course of action as such.

The real problem

These younger widows have too much time on their hands, being idle and gadding around from house to house (verse 13), perhaps 'from one house church to another'. Worse, some have been led astray and are meddling with the occult. Initially *gossips and busybodies* sounds faintly humorous, but these harmless translations conceal something more sinister. Gossip means talking foolish nonsense and gibberish may refer to repetitious nonsense syllables used in mystery religions (see 1:6; 6:20).

Busybodies is an uglier description. The related word in Acts 19:19 refers to magic arts in Ephesus. It could be translated as 'pryers into magic' or 'dabblers in the occult'. This ties in with some having turned away to follow Satan (verse 15: implicit in 2:14 and explicit in 4:1). Similar problems existed in neighbouring churches: Smyrna, Pergamum, Thyatira and Philadelphia (Revelation 2:9, 13, 24; 3:9). This trend may have been a hangover from traditional folk beliefs, but it was a Satanic attack upon the young churches. We can see why false teachers, both men and women, had to be silenced (1:3; 2:12). The survival of the apostolic gospel was at stake.

The solution

How could single women be kept from idleness? It was almost impossible for single women to be independent through honest work. They either had to marry or dedicate themselves completely to the service of the church. *So I counsel younger widows to marry, to have children, to manage their homes.* To us today this may sound like a sexist stereotyping of roles. However in New Testament times for lone women in the prime of life this was the only wise course: children and home will absorb surplus energy. Before the days of birth control, with a new baby every couple of years, to be fully employed with home tasks was the norm. The counsel Paul gives here is not at odds with his advice in 1 Corinthians 7:2, 'let each have her own husband' and in the context of widows, 'it is better to marry than to burn'. Paul is responding to false views of sex and celibacy. He is being consistent, even if at first sight verse 14 seems the very opposite of 1 Corinthians 7:8! He does say 'if her husband dies, she is free to marry anyone she wishes, but he must belong to the Lord' (1 Corinthians 7:39). This shows us that some words of Scripture address specific local situations. *Give the enemy no opportunity for slander* (verse 14). Paul is often concerned about the church's reputation with outsiders (2:2; 3:7; 6:1).

Questions

1. Many societies have seen a great increase in the number of single parents (mostly mothers) bringing up children. What does this passage suggest should be our Christian response?
2. Who is responsible for people's welfare? Themselves alone? Their families? The church? The state? In what proportion? Arrange these in order as a safety net for needy people.
3. Some churches treat marriage as the norm. How does this leave older single women? Feeling the church has no place for them and no work for them to do? Marginalized and

underemployed? How do single people react to 'family services'? How can they be helped to feel part of the family?

Widows in the Bible

The Bible has much to say about widows. In the Old Testament again and again Israel was told to care for widows and orphans. There are thirteen references in the Law (for example, Deuteronomy 10:18; 24:17). Elijah stayed with the widow of Zarephath, provided her needs miraculously and healed her son (1 Kings 17:9ff). The Book of Ruth tells us how three women reacted to becoming widows: with bitterness, by remarrying and by patient waiting. The Lord is declared to be the 'defender of widows' (Psalm 68:5) and he pleads 'the cause of widows' (Isaiah 1:17).

In the New Testament there are twenty-six references, nine in Luke's Gospel and nine in Paul's letters. Jesus condemns those who devour widows' houses (Matthew 23:14); commends the widow giving her mite (Mark 12:42); speaks of the widow to whom Elijah was sent (Luke 4:25); raised the widow's son at Nain (Luke 7:12). Acts 6:1 speaks of some widows being neglected. Mary, the mother of Jesus, was a widow. In Joppa they seem to have been a distinct group (Acts 9:39, 41) blessed by Dorcas' good works. Widows could live long lives – Anna (Luke 2:37) was widowed after seven years of marriage and was now eighty-four.

Men are more likely to die in warfare, and widowed men are more likely to remarry than women. Who provides for widows and orphans when the working man is dead? The dangers of exploitation and prostitution face them. James 1:27 makes caring for widows and orphans (what today we call 'single parents') a mark of true religion. The early church rose to such social responsibilities. And still today if you are female, and you marry, the probability is that you will spend your later years as a widow, so this is all very relevant!

1 Timothy 5:17–25

Elders good and bad

False teaching not only involved some widows, but also elders, who may need discipline and correction. Times have not changed!

 As with widows, Paul deals with deserving elders first, then turns to unworthy ones. *Elders* (verse 17) refers nowadays to a church office, not just older people. This is the first specific use of the word in the Pastoral letters, though we have seen that the word is interchangeable with 'overseer' (Acts 20:28; Titus 1:5).

Direct the affairs means to stand in front, lead or preside (see Romans 12:8; 1 Thessalonians 5:12). *Double honour* might mean twice the allowance a widow gets, or both money and respect for their office. It seems that while all elders direct the church's affairs, only some engage in preaching and teaching: some have verbal gifts and others nonverbal gifts as God himself determines (1 Corinthians 12:6, 11). 'Labour' is a favourite word of Paul's for his own apostolic labours (1 Corinthians 15:10), but he also uses it as here of elders and of the labours of four women workers (Romans 16). Our modern system often assumes ministers can exercise leadership because they have studied theology in college, whereas we want to insist that both teaching and ruling gifts come from the Spirit.

The *ox ... treading out the grain*, a quotation from Deuteronomy

105

25:4, is an example of a type of argument the rabbis used which moved from the lesser to the greater. If God cares for cattle how much more will he provide for his human servants. *For Scripture says* ... Paul uses the same quotations in 1 Corinthians 9:9–14. *The worker deserves his wages.* These words appear in Luke 10:7. Is Paul quoting Luke's Gospel already as being 'Scripture'? Luke may already have drafted his gospel while Paul was in prison in Caesarea, but at that time Scripture was the Old Testament only.

Unworthy elders

In any church charges can be made against leaders by dissatisfied members. Frivolous criticisms may be ignored, but strong measures must be taken when there is clear evidence of failure. The New Testament churches followed the Old Testament principle of requiring two or three witnesses before charges could be considered (verse 19: compare Deuteronomy 17:6; 19:15; Matthew 18:16; John 8:17; 2 Corinthians 13:1). Church leaders must be protected from malicious cranks and mischievous accusers. However, 'from among your own number' (Acts 20:30) shows that this was a live issue in Ephesus where false teachers were 'distorting the truth'.

Those who sin (verse 20). Those 'who persist in sinning' and will not listen to reason are to be publicly rebuked before the whole congregation. It is a momentous decision, almost impossible in 'shame cultures' where such public disgrace might mean a person never being seen again. *Publicly* 'before the other elders', so that other elders may take warning.

Paul gives Timothy a solemn charge (verse 21), perhaps because he shrank from confronting people, as we all do, or because he was tempted to show favouritism. He should be just and fair, not hasty in the laying on of hands; only appointing people as elders after careful scrutiny of their fitness for office; not rushing to reinstate those who had been rebuked or had repented. Delay is not usually harmful, whereas wrong appointments can do enormous damage. We carry the can for those we appoint (i.e., we share in the sins of others, verse 22). Bad appointments bring our own judgment into question, and the church loses credibility. Our leaders are only human and need our prayers, affirmation and encouragement: they can be tempted and have feet of clay. Timothy is commanded to be pure (verse 22), that is, to be above reproach in his dealings. The leader who fails himself cannot credibly deal with others: for example, David failed to discipline his son Amnon because of his own known adultery (2 Samuel 13).

Paul's train of thought is hard to follow in verse 23: why is Timothy to drink wine? A little wine would ease Timothy's stomach complaint. But in view of repeated warnings not to love much wine would sensitive Timothy think that purity required him to be a total abstainer? Did even he fail to recognize that everything God created is good? The Nazirite vow (Numbers 6) which required total abstention, twice mentions purity. Timothy may have tended to be ascetic himself, especially as a mixed blood person seeking not to offend either Jews or Greeks. Note that Paul does not recommend miraculous healing, but the use of medicinal alcohol for his frequent illnesses.

After this brief personal advice, Paul seems to return to the appointment of elders. While some people's failures are obvious (verse 24), others conceal their sins, which show up later to embarrass and harm the church. This underlines the need for careful screening before appointing leaders (see 3.10: 'they must first be tested'). Happily, the same is true of good deeds (verse 25): some are obvious, but all will be revealed in the end.

Questions

1. How can we muzzle our local church 'oxen' (leaders)? Do we pay them enough money and proper respect for their office? Do we expect greater sacrifice of them than we ask of ourselves?
2. If a church leader is accused of moral failure today, how would you apply these verses to their situation?

3. How should we respond when churches are criticized for the moral failure of church leaders destroying our credibility?

Comparison of the concerns regarding women in chapters 2 and 5

1 Timothy 2

9 'I want women to dress modestly with decency and propriety, not with braided hair or gold or pearls or expensive clothes'

10 'but with good deeds, appropriate for women who profess to worship God'

11 'A woman should learn in quietness and full submission'

12 'I do not permit a woman to teach or to have authority over a man; she must be silent.'

14 'Adam was not the one deceived; it was the woman who was deceived (by Satan)'

15 'But women will be saved through childbearing if they continue in faith, love and holiness with propriety'

1 Timothy 5

6 'the widow who lives for pleasure is dead even while she lives'

13 'they get into the habit of being idle'

10 'well known for her good deeds ... all kinds of good deeds'

13 'gossips and busy-bodies, saying things they ought not to'

15 'Some have in fact already turned to follow Satan'

14 'I counsel younger widows to marry, to have children'

The tone seems much the same, suggesting that the issues dealt with in the two chapters are related.

108

COPING WITH MARKET FORCES

1 Timothy 6

1 Timothy 6:1–2

Some words for the under class

Not only must widows and elders be respected (5:3, 17), but Christian slaves must respect their owners and not take liberties if they are working for fellow believers.

Paul begins with a command to all slaves to respect their masters, whether their employers are Christians or not. Slaves made up 50% of society in Greek cities, and churches may have had a higher proportion than that (see 1 Corinthians 1:26). Slaves were not just drudges and domestics, but included teachers and doctors, often better educated than their owners.

Under the yoke reminds us that slaves were disposable assets, little better than cattle. This was hard for any person to bear, but harder still for educated slaves, especially if they were Christians and even elders. Verse 1, continuing from chapter 5, might mean *All those* (elders) *who are under the yoke of slavery*. New freedom in Christ is no reason to be disrespectful to masters which could provoke employers to be hostile to the gospel.

So that God's name and our teaching may not be slandered. The overriding concern is how society will view the church, and therefore God. The same thinking should guide Christian employees today to respect their boss, not because the boss is always worthy of it, but as a witness that we serve Christ. Our behaviour at work can influence how they will think of God and his church.

Next we come to an even more delicate issue. How do Christian slaves relate to their Christian owners? In Christ they are brothers and sisters, who break the same bread and share the same cup. But being equal before God does not wipe out normal civil distinctions. Christian slaves must not expect to be let off if they are lazy or excused if they deserve a flogging. They are not to show less respect but to serve them even better. These verses apply today to all employed by fellow-Christians. Those employed by churches or parachurch societies may be tempted to treat their superiors in an offhand way. For example, Christian kids at school must not take advantage of the fact that their teacher attends the same church, and expect preferential treatment, or address them by Christian names, when everyone else uses 'Mr' or 'Sir'. *These are the things you are to teach and urge on them* refers to what has gone before (see 3:14; 4:6, 11; 5:7, 21; it is easy to miss these 'stage directions'). They tie together the whole practical section, before resuming the attack on the false teachers.

Questions

1. List those people to whom you personally owe respect. In what ways do you need to change your attitude or relationship?
2. How far does paying someone for their services reduce respect for them? How does this apply to church ministers?
3. How far is the church a witness to God's values, and how far a laughing stock in today's increasingly egalitarian society?

Slaves in Scripture

The New Testament says almost as much about slaves as widows (see 1 Corinthians 7:21–23; Galatians 3:28; Ephesians

6:5–9; Colossians 3:22–25; 1 Timothy 6:1–2; Titus 2:9–10; 1 Peter 2:18–25). The book of Philemon is about a runaway slave, Onesimus, from Colosse. The Law of Moses gave human rights to slaves: Sabbath rest, Jubilee release, freedom if badly treated, non-return if they escaped and death for slave traders! On the other hand, the Romans gave them few human rights: they could own nothing, their marriages had no legal status and their witness in court was only accepted if given under torture. In view of the cruelty and injustice of the Roman system, we may be surprised that in the New Testament there is no attack upon slavery as such, although 1:10 lumps together slave dealers with adulterers. Does this mean that God approved of slavery? Not at all: he liberated Israel from being slaves in Egypt. It was Christians, Livingstone, Mackay, Wilberforce and others in the 19th century, who brought the system down in the end.

1 Timothy 6:3–10

Religious people who love money

False teaching leads to friction and controversy. False teachers are motivated by desire for financial gain, the love of money.

Paul shifts his focus from Timothy teaching truth and returns to his offensive against those teaching error in the Ephesian church. They were people who do *not agree to the sound instruction* (healthy words) *of our Lord Jesus Christ*. This could refer to an early collection of Jesus' sayings (see 5:18; Acts 20:35). Good teaching is:

▶ Health giving

▶ Centres on Jesus

▶ Promotes a life of moral excellence.

By contrast, an acute description of what a bad teacher does:

▶ He thinks he has superior knowledge (inside information) but understands nothing worth knowing.

▶ He has an unhealthy or 'sick' interest in stirring up quarrels and divisions.

▶ He promotes *malicious talk* and *evil suspicions*. Paranoid hostility makes us try to blacken the names of those we disagree with by innuendoes and sarcasm.

▶ He constantly rubs people up the wrong way (*friction*).

▶ He produces the stench of *corrupt* (decaying) minds by depriving people of the truth.

All this is in the name of 'godliness' (verse 5). How can such a warped picture of true religion gain ground, as it did in Paul's day and surely does today? The answer lies in one word 'money' or *financial gain*. These people *think that* ('calculate', the same word is used of the vineyard workers in Matthew 20:10; and Simon Magus in Acts 8:20) here is a source of profit, a way of making money. Paul is not opposed to people being rich (verses 17–19), but to greed concealing itself under a cloak of religious belief, using Christian ministry as a way of becoming rich.

The Greeks were spellbound by the spoken word. Some philosophers were employed as tutors (Aristotle); some begged for a living (Diogenes); some supported themselves by working (like Paul) and some charged fees. Oratory became a racket to make money. Still today fringe groups use religion as a means to make money. Parasitic industries advertise in Christian magazines. We must take such warnings seriously. It would be tragic if Christian work was as well paid as secular work, it could attract people with impure motives. Paul was able to speak to the Ephesian elders (Acts 20:33–35) from a secure position, because they all knew he had made no money from working among them.

Contentment with bare necessities

But godliness with contentment is great gain. It really is. Paul wrote, 'I have learned to be content whatever the circumstances' (Philippians 4:11). 'Content' is a Stoic word for self-sufficiency, which is taught also in the New Testament (Luke 3:14; Hebrews 13:5). The Japanese samurai picked his teeth even when he hadn't eaten for three days. If he was hungry he would not show it! We must be content with whatever God chooses to provide. Stoic, Christian and Samurai all know that it is not what we possess, but an inward attitude of heart that makes us content. This is not a popular view today, even among some Christians, or those teaching 'Prosperity theology'. *For we brought nothing into the world and we can take nothing out of it.* Verse 7 brings us down to earth with its reminder of Job 1:21 (just as 5:18 quotes an Old Testament verse followed by a saying of Jesus, here too, after quoting the Old Testament, Paul alludes to Matthew 6:25 and Luke 12:22). The simple lifestyle, if we have food and clothing (quoting Deuteronomy 10:18), is taught by Jesus (Matthew 6: 24–34). Did Paul just pull all this teaching out of his own head? No, he built it all upon a passage in Ecclesiastes 5:10–20. Scripture is to be our guide.

The results of greed for money

The opposite of contentment is greed. Paul is not discussing the motives of the secular world here: *people who want to get rich* (verse 9) refers to religious workers. This desire for money is a snare used by the devil to entrap Christians, putting us into spiritual peril (see 3:7; 2 Timothy 2:26). Such greed springs from mindless and irrational desires that plunge or swamp people like a monstrous crocodile, which seizes its victim and drags it down to drown in destruction. *Some people, eager for money* have not only wandered from the faith but *pierced themselves with many griefs* (verse 10). These thorns of remorse and disillusion remind me of the rattan thorns that cling and rip the skin in secondary jungle. It is suicidal to love money. It is ironic that the desire for security ends in worry and anxiety. This is not a cautionary tale about some fictional character (e.g., Susan Howatch's, *The Rich are Different*, Penguin, 1989): it actually happened to leaders of the Ephesian church, and to many others since that time. Peter said to Simon Magus, 'May your money perish with you' (Acts 8:20). Paul speaks of 'enemies of the cross of Christ. Their destiny is destruction, their god is their stomach...their mind is on earthly things' (Philippians 3:18–19). Love of money leads to ruin.

Questions

1. What dangers await those who are determined to become rich? What positive attitude towards belongings is commanded for Christians?
2. How can we ensure that people do not make money out of religion in our community?
3. What does this passage have to say to those who teach 'prosperity theology', the belief that God rewards his children in this life with possessions and even riches?

The root of all evil?

An old popular song parodied this passage saying, 'Money is the root of all evil, take it away, take it away!' But Paul is not blaming money itself, but the love of money (literally 'love of silver', which was relevant in Ephesus, city of silversmiths). It is those who lust after profit and dedicate their energies to amassing capital who throw themselves open to evil.

The emphatic first word of this secular proverb is 'root'. It may mean 'a root' or 'the root' of *all kinds of evil* (and not the only root of all evil). The false teachers' love of money was mixed with Ephesian folk religion. All folk religions pursue health, wealth, good luck and general prosperity, trying to manipulate spiritual 'powers' to do what we want. Bringing together Christian faith and money-making is a danger still in some wealthy nations.

1 Timothy 6:11–16

Paul's personal charge to Timothy

Timothy is challenged to flee from loving money and pursue a holy, godly life. The Christian leader cannot evade this charge before God, who gives us life, and Christ Jesus our coming Lord.

Every time Paul speaks out against the false teachers he follows it up with direct words to Timothy to be different from them (see 2 Timothy 3:10, 14; 4:5).

Flee, pursue, fight and take hold (verses 11–12)

Paul gives these four commands to Timothy, whom he calls *man of God*, a title given in the Old Testament to God's agents, Moses, Samuel, Elijah, Elisha and David, a noble company indeed!

▶ *Flee*, run away as fast as you can from all this sordid desire for money. It needs a vigorous effort to escape its entanglements. We remember Joseph fleeing from Potiphar's wife (Genesis 39:12). Notice that love of money is placed alongside other threats to consistent Christian living. The New Testament also tells us to flee from:

    The evil desires of youth (2 Timothy 2:22)

    Sexual immorality (1 Corinthians 6:18)

    Idolatry (1 Corinthians 10:14).

▶ *Pursue*, run as fast as you can in the opposite direction, chasing after virtues. In contrast to vices that mark spiritual bankrupts, Paul lists six virtues that Timothy is to chase after (compare the list of nine in Galatians 5:22–23): righteousness, godliness, faith, love, endurance and gentleness. The last is a fruit of the Spirit and is a characteristic of Jesus himself (2 Corinthians 10:1). We must measure our lives against these lists of New Testament virtues and run for them.

▶ *Fight the good fight of the faith* (verse 12). This is not the military battle referred to in 1:18 but Paul's favourite athletic metaphor, following naturally after the idea of 'running' away and 'running' after. The agonized face of the athlete running the marathon illustrates the emphasis on continuing to contend.

▶ *Take hold*, however, points to a single once-for-all grasping or appropriating of eternal life: it is not earned by long-term performing of good deeds, but by a single act of accepting God's gift of salvation and eternal life. We may be pursuing virtues, which we have not yet fully achieved, but we have already grasped eternal life and will never let it go.

Note: The *good confession in the presence of many witnesses* might refer to Timothy's baptism in Lystra (Romans 10:9), or to his ordination (see 1:18), or his trial before imprisonment (Hebrews 13:23). Verse 13 hints that a trial is in Paul's mind but presumably Timothy had grasped eternal life from the time of his conversion. We need to 'grasp' eternal life at every major event of our lives.

Paul's solemn charge (verses 13–14)

In the sight of God...I charge you is a very solemn command. This was no pastime or picnic that Timothy was embarking upon. By nature a timid individual, he needed this kind of backbone-stiffening reminder and doctrinal encouragement. Paul calls upon the all-seeing God who gives life to everything. This possibly recalls the spiritual life given at baptism to the confessing candidate, though *Christ Jesus . . . testifying before Pontius Pilate* may rather hint at confessing before a Roman court.

This commandment (verse 14) could mean 'this letter' but is more likely to mean the whole law of God. Timothy, and ourselves as readers of this letter, are responsible for being faithful to the whole truth revealed in Scripture all our lives until the appearing of our Lord Jesus Christ. In the Pastorals this word 'appearing' is preferred to the word for 'royal visit' used in Paul's earlier letters. Both words were used in the imperial cult of the 'semi-divine' Roman emperor.

A glorious outburst of praise to God (verses 15–16)

Paul often leaps into a 'doxology' or shout of praise. For those who wish to be rich but are not, God's dazzling light shows how shabby and stupid it is to live for the cold glitter of gold and silver. 'You cannot worship God and money' Jesus said. In worshipping God, Paul uses language from both the secular and religious history of Israel:

▶ *King of kings* was used of Babylonian and Persian rulers (as in Ezekiel 26:7 and Daniel 2:37).

► *Lord of lords* was used of Israel's God in Deuteronomy 10:17 and Psalm 136:3 (and later of Christ in Revelation 17:14).

► *Who alone is immortal* is used in 1 Corinthians 15:53, 54 and in the doxology of 1 Timothy 1:17 as well.

► *Lives in unapproachable light* points to the 'Shekinah' glory of God (Exodus 24:15; 1 Kings 8:11; Psalm 104:2; Ezekiel 1:4).

► *No-one has seen or can see* recalls Exodus 33:20 and Isaiah's vision (6:5): 'Woe is me … my eyes have seen the King …'

How could anyone be so foolish as to exchange God's dazzling radiant glory for the pale gleam of gold? In the presence of such as God, this charge must be obeyed. He is to be royally served and his return in glory awaited. It is never money, but his majesty that motivates us for Christian service. How good is the God we adore! How glorious he is! How powerful these New Testament Scriptures are, as they build upon the Old Testament revelation.

Questions

1. What are the temptations you personally need to 'run to escape' from? How do you propose to set about doing it?
2. What are our motives for Christian service? To help the minister? To keep up appearances before the church? To keep in with God? Any others? Discuss this honestly.
3. Collect as many of the titles used in these Pastoral Letters as you can: use them in a time of praise together.

1 Timothy 6:17–21

Advice to those who are already rich

If you are already rich, don't worry, but do not put your trust in your wealth. Use it generously in Christ's service.

After the doxology, further discussion of money seems like an anticlimax. But there was a problem. Not all Christians in Ephesus were slaves: some people were wealthy citizens. The early church was dependent on rich people opening their spacious homes for church meetings. Such rich believers could have misunderstood Paul's strong words about the folly of trying to become rich. Today, Christians who are relatively well off can feel guilty when they reflect on the poverty and starvation in the world, especially when they hear words like those of Jesus to the rich young ruler, 'Sell everything you have and give to the poor, and you will have treasure in heaven' (Luke 18:22). Not all are called like Francis of Assisi to give everything away and live as a beggar. Paul does not suggest this. The rich have two responsibilities which poor people do not: negatively, to avoid arrogance and reliance on their wealth; and positively, to be generous and rich in doing good to those in need.

This paragraph (verses 17–21) is a single sentence in the original Greek, with a word play on 'riches' which is used in four ways: 'the rich', 'riches', an adverb 'richly' and a verb 'to be rich'. Thus rich people are not to trust in riches, but in God who richly gives all things and to be rich in good deeds! Paul then issues two commands.

Avoid the perils of the rich (verse 17)

It is easy for the rich to become arrogant, assuming a superior attitude over those who are less well off, especially if they are slaves (see Romans 12:16).

A parallel temptation is to rest on the security given by possessions, feeling comfortable that, if all else fails, at least one has a healthy bank balance. So the bank subtly usurps the place that God alone should occupy. How reliable is your bank? Even an apparently stable bank can collapse. God is not subject to stock market variations or devaluing currencies. Whether we are relatively rich or poor our confidence must be in God (Philippians 4:19).

This thought of God's provision for us leads to another aspect of God's goodness: *God, who richly provides us with everything for our enjoyment* (verse 17). Paul has touched on this before (4:3–4). This is a potent antidote to the error of the ascetic who believes enjoyment is unspiritual. God not only gives us life (verse 13) but makes it pleasant and enjoyable (Ecclesiastes 5:19–20). Our Lord is not a killjoy, spoilsport God who frowns and scowls. 'He provides you with plenty of food and fills your hearts with joy', Paul tells the pagans of Lystra (Acts 14:17). Christian faith is not world-denying, but world-transfiguring.

Fulfil the duties of the rich (verse 18)

Paul's second command is a reminder that being well off carries with it responsibilities. Four phrases, using words found only here in the New Testament, describe the proper lifestyle for the rich.

▶ *Do good* as God does (Acts 14:17). He does good: be like him.

▶ *Be rich in good deeds,* that is beautiful actions.

▶ *Be generous,* impart to others in bountiful fashion.

▶ *Be willing to share,* a phrase related to the word for a business partner.

These phrases are a delightful piling up of biblical attitudes to our material wealth and what to do with it. When Sir John Laing, founder of the international construction firm, died he left only a few hundred pounds. The rest of his money he used to endow a fund now amounting to millions, which brings help to churches. This is an example of amassing capital in the bank of heaven: deposit it there by giving it away here! This gives them and us a firm foundation for the coming age. The word 'foundation' can also mean a 'fund' as in English.

It is instructive to contrast the craving and desire for riches which results in destruction (verse 9) with the generous and openhanded use of wealth that provides a firm foundation for life that is truly life (verse 19). Money has great potential for good and evil. Where do we invest our capital? That is the issue here.

Closing encouragement (verses 20–21)

Paul ends his first letter to Timothy with words of warning and encouragement. Dealing with false teaching is distressing, but it has to be done, so get on with your job, Timothy!

The 'deposit' (verse 20: see also 2 Timothy 1:12) which has been entrusted to your care is the revealed truth of the gospel of Christ and must be guarded against falsehood. This secure, reliable body of truth is the opposite of the false teaching that has been the central theme of this letter and is summarized here:

▶ *Godless chatter* ('empty noise' see comments on 1:6 and 5:13).

▶ *Opposing ideas*, probably arguments between Old Testament Law and the gospel.

▶ *Falsely called knowledge.* Every few years someone crops up who wants to tell us 'the real truth', some fresh new understanding, which excites people to start with and then sadly becomes sectarian and divisive.

▶ *Wandered away.* This is where Paul started (see 1:6, 19). See how the whole letter ties neatly together round this theme.

Note: *Grace be with you* is not singular (as though addressed to Timothy alone), but plural, addressed to all believers in Ephesus. Paul expected the whole church would read this letter sent to Timothy, understand its concerns and obey its message.

The letter is not a random connection of unrelated, scattered thoughts about church order, loosely strung together, but a closely knit message aimed at an actual crisis situation. It is a 'theology of the street', a dispatch written in the heat of battle for the truth over against the false teaching of Ephesian folk religion. False teaching continues to poke up its evil head today and this letter remains a potent weapon with which to fight it.

Questions

1. How can we avoid being arrogant and despising others less blessed than we are?
2. Compare the two sections on wanting to be rich (verses 6–10) and being rich (verses 17–19). How do they help us in deciding how to use our resources, great or small, for God's greatest glory?
3. How far should a rich Christian pay the expenses of his or her local church? What effect would this have on other members?

Where did New Testament churches meet?

Excavations in the ruins of Ostia, sixteen miles from Rome, reveal a community of about 27,000 people. There were some thirty-three detached mansions, some luxury three-room apartments in four-storey buildings, and the rest lived in small one-room homes. The largest house could take nine people reclining in the dining-room (see 1 Corinthians 11:21) and perhaps as many as fifty sitting in the open courtyard or garden called the atrium. This suggests churches were dependent upon rich citizens with larger households to be their patrons. This explains the roles of Phoebe (Romans 16:1–2), Aquila and Priscilla, Lydia, Nympha (Colossians 4:15), Philemon and Gaius (Romans 16:23). They must have been owners of houses large enough to 'host' a congregation.

A TASK FOR
TITUS IN CRETE

Titus 1

Introduction to Titus

Background

Some facts about Crete

Crete is an island 152 miles long, varying from 7 to 32 miles in width, and with mountains up to 8000 ft (2425m), largely of bare limestone, honeycombed with caves and liable to earthquake. It lies across the southern entrance to the Aegean Sea, a convenient landfall for seafarers.

The Minoan culture of the Bronze Age was centred on Knossos. Cretans not only spread around the Aegean Sea, but from there the 'Sea Peoples' (including the Philistines), migrated to the eastern end of the Mediterranean. After being repulsed by Egypt they built five city states (Gath, Askelon, Ashdod, Ekron and Gaza) on the coastal plain, which is still called Palestine after the Philistines. Through the prophet Amos (9:7) the Lord says 'Did I not bring Israel up from Egypt, the Philistines from Caphtor and the Arameans from Kir?' God overruled the migration of Philistines from Caphtor (Crete). The Kerethites of King David's bodyguard (2 Samuel 15:18) were native-born Cretan mercenaries. Crete was annexed by the Romans in 67 BC.

Some Cretans were present on the Day of Pentecost (Acts 2:11), but we do not know if they started any churches there. The mission of Paul and Titus to Crete is thus a mission to 'Caphtor', the original Philistine homeland. These warlike people were never outside the providence and mercy of God, who had overruled their eastward migration. Now their opportunity had come: 'this gospel must first be preached to all nations and then will the end come' (Matthew 24:14).

Paul's visits to Crete

Consult an atlas and you will see that Crete is a port of call on any eastbound voyage from Italy, a 'Gateway to the Aegean'. We know that Paul's ship had called at a central port on the south coast, Fair Havens, on his way, as a prisoner, to Rome (Acts 27:7–13). But it seems unlikely he would have had time to plant churches then. We must assume that Paul had been released from house arrest in Rome, abandoning his earlier plans to go to Spain (Romans 15:28) and deciding instead to revisit the province of Asia (writing to Philemon in Colosse: 'Prepare a guest room for me, because I hope to be restored to you in answer to your prayers': Philemon 22). Accompanied by Titus, he had subsequently preached Christ in Crete.

The possible scenario is this: Paul and Titus evangelized towns and planted churches in Crete. Then Paul went on to Ephesus, leaving Titus behind to 'follow up'. In Ephesus Paul found error rampant in the church, kicked out two elders guilty of false teaching and left Timothy behind to mop up the mess. Having moved on and written his first letter to strengthen Timothy's hand, Paul realized that Titus might be facing similar issues, made worse by the Cretan character and many Jewish converts. So he wrote a similar, but briefer letter to Titus, to confirm his earlier verbal instructions in writing.

The letter

The letter outlines what Titus is to teach the Cretan churches. We can apply it to our own lifestyles as church members today. Titus reads like a muted digest of 1 Timothy. Apart from the opening paragraph (1:1–4) and closing greetings (3:12–15) only the teaching passages (2:11–14) and (3:3–7) cannot be matched in 1 Timothy. The letter has only 46 verses as against 113 in 1 Timothy. The main emphasis is upon 'beautiful deeds', a winsome lifestyle, as a way to reduce prejudice and refute slanders against the church.

An outline of Titus's ministry

▶ *Test-case:* a Gentile Christian not compelled to be circumcised (Galatians 2:1–3).

▶ *Emissary* sent by Paul to Corinth (2 Corinthians 2:13; 7:6, 13, 14; 8:6, 16, 17, 23; 12:18).

▶ *Follow up man* left behind to follow up Paul's Cretan campaign (Titus 1:5).

▶ *Colleague* urged to rejoin Paul at Nicopolis, on the Greek west coast (Titus 3:12).

▶ *Pioneer* to Dalmatia, further north in former Yugoslavia (2 Timothy 4:10).

In the New Testament Titus first appears in Jerusalem with Paul and Barnabas (Galatians 2:1, 3). He was a pure-blooded Greek, who was never circumcised, unlike Timothy, whose mother was Jewish. Why is Titus never mentioned in Acts, though he was Paul's trusted troubleshooter in Corinth and Crete? One possible explanation is that he was Luke's brother! Luke wrote Acts but never mentions himself specifically. If Titus was his brother he would probably have left him out too. There is no compelling evidence of this relationship but it is a possibility.

Titus seems to have been a tougher man than Timothy. Paul gave him demanding assignments to the Corinthians, the Cretans and the Dalmatians. You could call him Paul's follow-up man or troubleshooter! He seems to have been a man of unusual tact, possessing great gifts of leadership. Cretans today remember him as 'Bishop Titus' or 'St Titus' and the absence of venomous snakes on the island is attributed to him!

Titus 1:1–4

Opening greeting

The brief greeting which begins all letters enlarges into a summary of the gospel.

 These four verses (a single sentence in the original Greek) are not just a pious, long-winded opening from the ageing apostle. These verses already hint at the issues to be raised in the letter.

First of all, Paul establishes his own credentials (verse 1), chiefly in order to give his authority to Titus in dealing with the Cretans. At first sight *servant* or slave may not seem to be an impressive or authoritative title, but 'Slave of God' is an honourable title used of Moses and Joshua (Joshua 1:1–2; 24:29) and the prophets (Jeremiah 7:25; Amos 3:7), and claimed by many New Testament writers: Paul (Romans 1:1); James (1:1); Peter (2 Peter 1:1); Jude (1:1) and John (Revelation 1:1).

Paul is also sent out as *an apostle of Jesus Christ,* the second Person of the Godhead. This is not just holy name-dropping. Paul had been given an awesome and authoritative commission (look at Acts 9:15–16; 26:16–18). *God's elect* (chosen one) is Old Testament language (Psalm 105:43; Isaiah 65:9, 15). Paul seems to borrow current jargon words: *knowledge* and *godliness.* *Knowledge of the truth* (see 1 Timothy 2:4) must blossom and fruit

129

into *godliness*, a major theme of this letter. This is the precise opposite of the result of the false teaching which was widespread in Crete (verses 10–16): these teachers' lies and deceit lead inevitably to corrupt behaviour. Even this opening greeting highlights issues the letter will deal with. In view of the Cretan reputation for lying (verse 12), describing God as the one *who does not lie* is very pointed (see Numbers 23:19).

Before the beginning of time

God's pre-cosmic plan, conceived before the world existed and outside of time itself, was that a chosen people, called out from many nations, should know the truth and live the truth. The scope of this canvas is immense. Crete boasted a long, glorious history going back to the Bronze Age (the Philistines conquered the Israelites because they obtained iron technology before anyone else). But God, who does not lie, had promised what was happening now, through Paul and Titus, before time even began! This solemn opening was intended to be read over Titus's shoulder by the Cretans (just as the Ephesians read 1 Timothy).

Titus, my true son is a title shared by Timothy (1 Timothy 1:2), suggesting Paul had led both to faith. How flexible Paul was: he circumcised Timothy (a father's role, Genesis 21:4); but Titus became a test-case of a Gentile Christian, baptized but left uncircumcised (Galatians 2:3). He was, nonetheless, Paul's true spiritual son, sharing the same faith, albeit a Gentile. If converted Jews were unwilling to accept Titus's ministry, because he was not Jewish, these words recommend Titus as 'kosher' and a real 'mensch'!

It is a tradition in many cultures that sons follow their father's trade, just as Jesus followed Joseph as a carpenter. Timothy and now Titus are following in their (spiritual) father's footsteps, inheriting his delegated authority. *Common* is a word relating to a business partner, as in the Galilean fishery business in which the sons of Zebedee were Simon's partners (Luke 5:10). *Grace and peace* combines both Greek and Jewish greetings, like *selamat* (Malay) and *ping-an* (Chinese) in Malaysia. (Notice that Paul uses the word *Saviour* six times in this letter, twice in each chapter; three times it refers to God and three times to Jesus.)

Questions

1. How far is it possible to believe lies and live a good life? What truths are necessary to produce a godly life?
2. Together turn verses 1–3 into a hymn to use in your group or in the wider church. Enlist some musical talent if you can.
3. Reconsider Question 1 on a national and social scale. What leads to a law-abiding, well behaved society? More prisons? Better laws? Stricter enforcement? Better education? Or what?

Titus 1:5–9

The new eldership

Timothy replaced established elders in Ephesus. In Crete Titus appoints elders in newly-formed congregations.

Titus's task was twofold:

1. *Straighten out what was left unfinished* (verse 5). Perhaps a church had been started by Cretan Jews present at Pentecost, but it never got off the ground. Now Paul had conducted a successful mission, and follow-up is essential. A framework is needed for new plants to grow on. In either event, the way to put things in order is to appoint local leaders.

131

2. *Appoint elders in every town* (verse 5). Homer spoke of 'Crete of a hundred cities'. We do not know how many now boasted Christian communities, but clearly Titus did, and had already been directed by Paul what to do.

Elder (verse 5) and *overseer* (verse 7) mean the same. Paul appointed elders as early as possible in the life of a new church (Acts 14:21–23). If no elders had yet been appointed, the Cretan churches must have been young indeed. Was Titus the founding missionary, or the first 'bishop'? He was told not to leave until Artemas or Tychichus arrived (3:12), suggesting that his role was crucial.

Fifteen qualifications for elders are listed: only five use the same words as in 1 Timothy though another five are close. There seems a more ordered pattern here than in 1 Timothy: household matters are placed first, followed by five vices, then six virtues. Duties are spelt out in verse 9, so it is in part a job-description. Quick-tempered, greedy boozers with many other faults seem very common among the converts! In the original Greek the items in verse 6 appear in the form of questions: 'Is he without fault?' 'Does he have only one wife?' *etc.*, almost like interview questions to be asked of candidates.

Family status (verse 6)

Blameless means not liable to have charges brought against one. Being holy and blameless matters more than being faultlessly efficient. The candidate must have a blameless sexual life too and his family must set a good example (see notes on 1 Timothy 3:4). *Wild* means prodigal or spendthrift. *Disobedient* is used of Eli's sons (1 Samuel 2:12).

Christians learn leadership in their homes. This prepares them to be leaders in church. In the infant church, when church buildings were as yet unheard of, the householder would often be the leader of the church meeting in his home. The elder is the kind of person whose children follow on to become believers. He or she is God's household manager, a steward who belongs to

God *entrusted with God's work. An overseer* need not imply that each one must have all the abilities and gifts, but overseers between them should share these qualities.

Five vices the elders must not have (verse 7)

These brief lists of vices to avoid and virtues to be prized, have puzzled some commentators: the standards seem too low, more typical of unbelievers than Christian saints. But most pioneer missionaries today would laugh at this lack of realism. It's no use pitching standards so impossibly high as to discourage people. Modern books about Crete suggest things have not changed much in 2000 years! The five vices to avoid are:

▶ Being *overbearing*, that is, stubborn, pigheaded people who stick to their opinion no matter what good reasons are opposed to it. These first two words are not found in 1 Timothy 3. Were they inserted because of the Cretan character?

▶ Being *quick tempered*, easily aroused, remaining angered.

▶ *Given to drunkenness*, a heavy drinker overindulging in wine.

▶ Being *violent*, a giver of blows, a striker (find both in 1 Timothy 3:3).

▶ *Pursuing dishonest gain*. It was said of Cretans, 'They are so given to making gain in disgraceful and acquisitive ways that among the Cretans alone of all men, no gain is counted disgraceful' and, Cretans stuck to money like bees to honey!

Six virtues elders should have (verse 8)

Rather (verse 8), a very strong 'but', contrasts the vices with these virtues.

▶ *Hospitable* ('a lover of foreigners'), welcoming not only church members, but Christian travellers too (wayside inns were hotbeds of vice).

▶ *Loves what is good,* be enthusiastic for moral goodness, a major theme of this whole letter.

▶ *Self-controlled,* a favourite word in the Pastorals meaning 'having his wits about him', able to control one's passions.

▶ *Upright,* righteous or just.

▶ *Holy,* pious, respecting basic values.

▶ *Disciplined.* Self-control is the ninth fruit of the Spirit (Galatians 5:22).

A leader must have firm beliefs (verse 9)

Anybody in a position of leadership must have a clear grasp of the basic Christian truths. This is more than an ability to remember certain doctrines, sign a doctrinal statement, parrot them in an interview or regurgitate them for an examination. It is not enough to have attended a course or obtained a qualification by correspondence, however excellent. Leaders need to be enthusiasts for the truth, devoted to the gospel, with strong convictions and able to recognize deviations from biblical teaching. If they lack convictions their leadership will lack purpose and direction and the fellowship will be led round in circles. This is a stronger statement than elders being 'apt to teach' and deacons keeping 'hold of the deep truths of the faith' (1 Timothy 3:2, 9).

Elders have both a positive and a negative task.

▶ *To encourage others by sound doctrine,* teaching the health-giving words of the truth, which they have grasped for themselves.

▶ *To refute those who oppose it,* dealing with error. In 1 Timothy

Paul starts with the false teachers, and then goes on to the elders who must replace them. This letter to Titus starts with appointing elders and next turns to false teaching.

Questions

1. Go through Paul's list of virtues and vices. How blameless are you? (Be honest – don't assume you are guilty on all counts; nor are you perfect.)
2. Are your church leaders chosen for their gifts, their learning or their character? Which is most important? Why?
3. Is the quality of life expected of church leaders in the public eye too high or too low? Do we expect more from them than from ourselves? Why? How can we help them?

Titus 1:10–16

Dealing with false teachers

Jewish false teachers causing trouble *must be silenced* and the wild characteristics of native Cretans must be rebuked *sharply*.

The train of thought in this first chapter is simple: good leaders must be appointed to deal with chronic disorder, *for there are many rebellious people* (verse 10), that is, insubordinate, the opposite of being subject. It seems that there were many Jews in Crete (see Acts 2:11 and 1 Maccabees 15:23). *Especially* is to be understood to say 'in other words, I mean'.

Those of the circumcision group means converts from Judaism, who seem to have been a main source of trouble. They encouraged defiance of church leaders, calling their followers to reject gospel teaching. When people refuse to accept the authority of church leaders it results in disorder and hinders progress. These people *must be silenced* (verse 11) literally, muzzled, their mouths stopped: this is the most urgent note sounded in the whole letter. They were *ruining whole households* (house churches) by teaching things they *ought not to teach* (see comment on 1 Timothy 5:13 and Acts 19:17–20), perhaps a further veiled reference to magic arts and superstitions, *for the sake of dishonest gain.* Here is the money motive again (as in 1 Timothy 6:5–10). Besides the erroneous teaching of the Jewish-led opposition, the second fundamental problem arose from the Cretan character.

Human nature as found in Crete

Paul would have studied the Greek philosophers at school, as we study English literature and sometimes remember some of it! Here he quotes Epimenides of Knossos, a Cretan philosopher from around 600 BC whom Aristotle called a prophet (Paul quotes the same man in Acts 17:28, 'In him we live and move and have our being.'). 'Cretans are always liars, evil brutes, lazy gluttons.' (See also *The Cretan Character*, p. 138.) *This testimony is true.* Paul's cheerful agreement with this proverb shows down-to-earth realism.

Teaching Cretans to forsake their deeply engrained cultural values, and become consistent Christians, would be a tough assignment, even for Titus. While we are amused about the shortcomings of the Cretans, we should turn Paul's searchlight on ourselves. Inevitably we are all influenced and programmed by the culture in which we have grown up. All human nature is flawed and each culture has its own version of that corrupted nature. We have been so immersed in our own culture that we find it difficult even to see its shortcomings objectively, let alone repent of them. We need to ask those from other cultures to criticize us (though they are generally too polite). They may therefore need some prompting, but with the Holy Spirit's help we may discover some home truths about ourselves. But the Bible does not encourage cynical pessimism. Paul does not suggest that even the Cretans should be written off. The transforming power of the gospel can change them and us, if we pray for it.

Problems of teaching in the Cretan churches

Rebuke them sharply (verse 13) is good medical advice, *so that they will be healthy (sound)*. If Dr Luke wrote this letter at Paul's direction (see notes on 2 Timothy 4:11 and p. 37) it could explain this choice of words. Surgery is painful, but should result in better health. The knife was needed in four areas of the Cretan churches:

► *Jewish myths ... commands of those who reject the truth* (verse 14). Jewish religion accumulated rules as a ship grows barnacles (see Isaiah 29:13, quoted by Jesus himself: Matthew 15:8–9; Mark 7:6–7). Being obsessed with laws and rules blinds people to the gospel of grace. 1 Timothy 1:4; 4:7 shows that this was widespread.

► *Ritual purity* (verse 15). For those who insist on detailed observance of petty rules and regulations nothing can ever be really pure – there is always another new demand coming up. The teaching of Jesus (Mark 7:15, 20–23) is that it is not externals and what we eat which defile us, but inward defilement of our sinful human nature: and it is not ritual purification which cleanses us, but faith in the death of Christ and the cleansing applied by his Spirit.

► *Spiritual pride* (verse 16). *They claim to know God.* Jews made the proud claim that they knew God in a way that the Gentiles could not. Such an attitude persisting within the church would destroy it. Compare 1 Thessalonians 4:5;

Galatians 4:8, 9; Romans 2:17–24. Actions remain the acid test of reality. In Christ, Jews and Gentiles alike are sinners saved by God's grace, not by rules of the law.

▶ *Disobedience* (verse 16). They obey human commandments and disobey God's. They are unfit for 'good works' – again the theme of the letter – that is, godliness.

Paul goes on to detail the good works he is looking for. Titus must denounce Cretan lying and brutish gluttony on the one hand and Jewish pride in the Law on the other. If all believers automatically become good models of Christian perfection, there would be no work for pastors and elders to do! Titus had a huge task ahead of him in Crete.

Questions

1. Ask God to show you whether you have any cultural blind spots that require a change of behaviour.
2. How can a church fellowship decide the difference between its members' shortcomings (needing help and encouragement) and fundamental corruption (needing rebuking and silencing)?
3. What part did money play in the life of people in Crete? And in your own culture?
4. Paul would be accused of racism if he made these remarks today. In what circumstances do you think that modern Christian preachers should use this kind of language ever?

The Cretan character

Cretans were such notable liars that the Greeks coined a verb *kretizō* meaning to lie and cheat. The Cretans even tried to attract tourists by claiming that the tomb of Zeus was in Crete (after all, 'the gods' were supposed to be immortal!). The English word 'syncretism' also derives from Crete. The Cretan tribes were always fighting each other and could not live in peace, but on rare occasions the Cretans did cooperate to fight against a common enemy, an unlikely alliance known as 'syncretism' (a word devised by Plutarch according to the *International Bulletin of Missionary Research*, April 1992).

The Cretans had a bad press from another writer:

Cretans on account of their innate avarice live in a perpetual state of private quarrel and public feud and civil strife…you will hardly find anywhere characters more tricky and deceitful than those of Crete…money is so highly valued among them, that its possession is not only thought to be necessary, but highly creditable; and in fact greed and avarice are so native to the soil in Crete that they are the only people in the world among whom no stigma attaches to any sort of gain whatever.

(Polybius, *Polybius*, 6.46, Loeb edition)

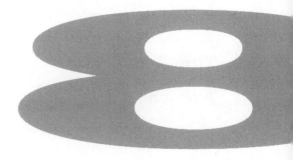

BLAMELESS LIVING

Titus 2

Titus 2:1–8

A teaching programme for young and old

The task facing Titus is basically a teaching job – new Christians shaped by traditional Cretan cultural values must be transformed by the Christian counterculture: from now on they must lead beautiful lives.

Notice that the words 'teach' and 'teaching' are found ten times in the NIV and the chapter begins and ends with this key idea – Titus's task is to teach! Like Timothy (1 Timothy  4:12) he, too, is to teach, not only in words but by example (verse 7). The NIV again omits the two little connecting words *But you* (verse 1) which clearly contrast Titus with the false teachers just discussed (1:10ff). We've just heard what *they* are teaching: now this is what *you* must teach!

Paul uses the same framework as 1 Timothy 5:1–2, enlarged and in different order, breaking down the 'school' into five 'classes': older men, older women, younger women, younger men and slaves.

The older men

'Older men' does not mean 'elders' here, though many elders would fall into this group. These are not just vague moral 'qualities' to be looked for – Paul is talking about real old Cretan men, sitting by the road, with craggy, lined faces. Look at it from the other end for a moment – what are the common failings of older men? They may be tempted to eat too much and get overweight (*lazy gluttons* 1:12); become dirty, untidy, confused and no longer *worthy of respect* (verse 2). They may lose control of bodily functions, but also of their feelings and become irritable and bad tempered: *Self-controlled* is the opposite of *evil brutes* (1:12). They may weaken in faith, becoming sour and cynical, self-centred and unloving. Losing the bright expectancy of youth, they become hard and brittle and resent every inconvenience. Thus they need to become *sound in faith, in love and in endurance* (the same three virtues expected of Timothy as 'man of God' (1 Timothy 6:11); of Paul (2 Timothy 3:10) and the Thessalonian Christians (1 Thessalonians 1:3).

Titus is expected to minister to all age groups in the church: it may seem easier to focus upon young people, but the ageing have their own pastoral needs.

The older women

Many of the weaknesses of older men are shared by older women, but Paul highlights positive and negative aspects of living as great-aunts and grannies. *Reverent in the way they live* translates two beautiful and rare words, meaning 'demeanour suited to consecration to the temple'. Older women are to see themselves as holy priestesses, like Anna (Luke 2:37) who 'never left the temple but worshipped night and day'.

After this lovely portrait of what older women are to be like, the two negatives which follow come as a shock. *Not slanderers.* The word in the singular means 'devil'. In the plural it means 'false accusers' just as the devil accuses Christians. Older people may be prone to find fault with others and criticize and blame them to all and sundry. *Not addicted to much wine.* Addiction to alcohol is not only a twentieth-century problem, nor is it restricted to Crete. Lonely women can still take refuge in the bottle. Older women must choose between becoming malicious, alcohol addicts, or holy, beautiful teachers. Titus is to face them with that choice!

The younger women

Titus must delegate the training of younger women to the older women. It may have been improper for Titus to train young women directly, and the older women would know more about women's lives than Titus anyway. This is another good reason for enlisting others to share in teaching (see notes on 2 Timothy 2:2). No one individual can hope to be competent in every sphere.

Younger women need to be trained to *love their husbands and children* (verse 4). In Ephesians 5:25 and 33 husbands are commanded to *love* their wives and wives to *respect* their husbands. Some suggest women don't need ordering to love their husbands, they will love them anyway, but that it's respecting them that is difficult! Yet here younger women, perhaps subject to arranged marriages, have to be trained to love husbands and children. Perhaps Cretan women were fierce with their husbands and lacked maternal affection. Clearly the Bible expects it. Timothy's mother and grandmother were model 'lovers of children'.

To be busy at home (verse 5) means to be 'workers at home' or 'domestic'. From our present-day perspective we may be tempted to write these words off, because they seem to imply the inferiority of women to men. But life was very different in first-century Crete. The alternative to being domestic was not having a career but behaving in an anti-social and dishonourable way, failing to realize how different life was in first-century Crete (See *Changing cultures* on p. 146).

All of this is so that the watching world (verse 5) will be impressed by Christians' home life and lifestyle, and unable to find any excuse there to *malign the word of God*. If Christian women traded on their newly-found equality in Christ, they might bring rebuke on the gospel. This is the first of many words about the need for beautiful deeds to impress outsiders.

Younger men

It is surprising that Paul has so little to say about the younger men – only one word, be *self-controlled* and it has already been used of older men and younger women. Yet if only the younger men of Crete could be self-controlled what an evidence for the reality of the gospel! If only these young *liars* and *evil brutes* could restrain their wildness! (Today motor insurance policies for young men are higher than for older people, because they are more likely to be involved in road accidents.) It may be that Titus was still in the 'younger man' age bracket so he must not merely talk to them (did talking to people ever do much good in curbing the headstrong?) but *set them an example* (verse 7). The teacher must be the model, as Greek philosophers were to their students. Christian leadership is not about bossing people around, but being an example *in everything*.

▶ Jesus was a model and example to his disciples (John 13:15).

▶ Elders were to be examples to the whole church (1 Peter 5:3).

▶ Timothy was to be an example to the church in Ephesus (1 Timothy 4:12).

What helps us most is being given a model to imitate. We shape our thinking about how Christians should live by learning how Christ lived and by watching fellow-Christians, rather than by hearing sermons. If a leader acts in certain ways, the rest of us feel it's OK to do the same even if standards are being lowered. This duty for Christian leaders is a heavy burden to bear.

Integrity means unspoiled by corruption, and is used of beautiful young virgins (Esther 2:2). Christian ministers are to be like unsullied virgins, not like professional harlots merely doing what they are paid for. No ammunition is to be given to critics.

Questions

1. If you are young, how do you get on with older people? How do you set about helping them? If you are old, how do you respond to Paul's directions? Refer back to verses 2 and 3.
2. How can modern young women understand verses 4 and 5 and find positive help from this teaching?
3. Can people be *trained* to love their relations? How could it be done? A blameless life reinforces the healthy words.

Changing cultures

Do changing cultures make 'subjection to husbands' irrelevant in today's world? Greek women remained in their own part of the house where they never met any men apart from their husbands. Their chief role was to be at home with the children. They never went out unaccompanied. Paul is encouraging Cretan women to live Christianly within their own culture.

It would have been nonsense to urge them to go out and get a career, pay off the mortgage or, if they didn't like their husbands, set up as single parents! But are there principles that we can apply in today's world? The basic principles are relevant in all societies: love; self-control; purity; kindness; relating appropriately to their husbands; giving love and security to the children. Young men and women look for many qualities in potential partners, but being *kind* is a crucial quality that makes a marriage work.

In English, phrases like *be subject to their husbands* and 'submission' carry undertones of cowed, cringing surrender. But (see note on 1 Timothy 2:11) the picture of church members relating like army units in order of battle, helps to solve the obvious question of how everyone can be mutually subject to everybody else. So translate it as 'take up their proper station in relation to their husbands'.

Titus 2:9–10

Christians who are slaves

This social group is a significant interface between the church and society.

This short section is fundamental to the effective outreach of the church. Though the first four groups seem to have covered all possible options slaves get special mention (see comments on 1 Timothy 6:1–2). More than 50% of the population of Greek cities were slaves and this despised social class seems to have been responsive to the gospel, probably making up a higher proportion of Christians than of the general population (the 'not many mighty' of 1 Corinthians 1:26). If citizens were to be won over it would be through the attractive witness of slaves in their daily work.

Jesus reminded his hearers that slaves cannot be at the total disposal of more than one master at a time (Matthew 6:24). *Please* is most often used of men pleasing God (Colossians 3:20; Philippians 4:18; Ephesians 5:10). The two commonest faults of slaves are *talking back*, feeling frustrated and angry, especially when punished (1 Peter 2:23), and *stealing*. People who own nothing are often tempted to pilfer, and help themselves when no-one is looking. Employers cannot always be searching their slaves. It's one thing to miss an item, and another to recover it.

This is why honest Christian slaves are appreciated. *Make attractive* or *Adorn* is the Greek word from which we derive 'cosmetic' though of course, Paul is not thinking of merely putting on a Christian face. He wants the slaves to be Christian through and through. Trustworthy Christian slaves (and employees) make the gospel winsome and credible. If we claim to have been saved by *God our Saviour* we should prove it in lives adorned with beautiful behaviour. This verse flows easily into the next section.

Questions

1. Make a list of people who might possibly look to you for an example of Christian living. It should include the people you work for and with. What do they see as they watch your life?
2. If the early church saw the witness of slaves as a key to outreach, how far are churches today neglecting the key role of Christians in the work place? We have Christian models in sport and showbusiness: how many in work and business?
3. Pilfering, corruption and fraud are commonplace in public life in all countries. What can we do about it?

Sound/healthy

This is a favourite 'Pastorals' word, being used in 2:1, *sound doctrine*, 2:2, *sound in faith* and 2:8, *soundness of speech*. This Greek medical word gives us the English 'hygiene'. Luke uses it in Luke 5:31, 'It is not the healthy who need a doctor, but the sick'; Luke 7:10, 'the men … found the servant well'; and Acts 4:10, 'It is by the name of Jesus Christ … that this man stands before you healed'.

Some scholars question whether Paul wrote the Pastorals because of the use of words not found in earlier letters, e.g., this word for 'sound. It is used nine times in the Pastorals, fifteen times in the gospels and Acts, and once in 3 John. We know, however, that Paul never personally wrote any of the letters that bear his name. Because of his eye problems someone else always wrote for him. When 2 Timothy was written 'only Luke is with me', so only he could have written that letter as Paul directed. Thus frequent use of medical words is not surprising. Though the word 'sound' was of medical origin, some philosophers began using such words generally, for example, accusing their critics of having sick minds; rotten ideas spreading like gangrene; just as Paul used them in the vivid language of the Pastorals. The word itself is a 'healthy' word – the Living God gives life to all he touches. Jesus' touch brought health to the man with leprosy; his word was enough to restore health to the man who had lain so long by the pool of Bethesda. Even after the Ascension his name was sufficient to cause the lame man at the Beautiful Gate to go leaping and dancing through the Gate into the inner courts. The teaching of the Bible gives health to all of us who read it and begin to share a biblical approach to this world.

Titus 2:11–15

Christ's beauty and the beast-ly Cretans

Why Christians should live beautiful pure and godly lives.

 This letter to Titus may seem like a shortened form of 1 Timothy, but the closing quarter of Titus 2 is packed with lovely statements found only in this letter. Paul gives four reasons why the Cretans and ourselves should live 'beautiful' lives, in fact he

gives the reasons for everything he has written so far.

Why should old men 'endure' and how? Why should old women keep off the bottle? Why should young women be good mothers, young men show restraint and slaves please their masters? What motivates us to live beautifully and how? The New Testament contains no Leviticus, no sets of rules (though well-meaning people always try to supply them!): rather the Bible gives us theological reasons why, motives for Christian ethics.

Jesus was born into our world

According to *the grace of God* our Saviour's great plan bringing *salvation* (verse 11), God has *appeared* in human history. He lived as the child of a young woman, was blessed by older men like Simeon and old women like Anna. He lived (and died) as a young man. Outside the Pastorals, the Greek word translated here as 'appeared' is found only in Acts 27:20 and Luke 1:78, where the picture is of sunrise bursting forth: 'the rising sun will come to us from heaven to *shine* on those living in darkness', pointing to God's decisive act: Jesus, 'the dayspring from on high has visited us!' The rising sun that the Japanese ignorantly worshipped is thus declared. *The grace of God that brings salvation* is a lovely Christmas text to describe Christ being born as a human baby. In this context *all men* could mean old and young, men and women. To walk in this light means *to say 'No' to ungodliness and worldly passions*. This implies 'renounce once for all', as in the Anglican Catechism: 'renounce the Devil and all his wicked works'. So the first reason for godly living is that Christ has brought us light to show us how to live and give us power to live. The shining light of God's grace in Jesus dawns in our hearts, transfiguring our lives, making them beautiful.

Jesus will come back to our world a second time

The second reason for living good and pure lives is that Jesus has promised to return – *the glorious appearing of our great God and Saviour, Jesus Christ* (verse 13). The second *appearing* of Jesus, at an unknown and unexpected future time, will be glorious, dramatic and the consummation of world history (see Matthew 24, especially verses 14, 30–31, 36). He will come to receive his own people, but will also come to judge everyone, not only evildoers and atheists, but the family of God (2 Corinthians 5:10; 1 Peter 4:17). For those who look forward to his return, here is another motive for living good lives: what will he find us doing when he returns (Matthew 24:45–51; 2 Peter 3:11–12)?

Jesus died to redeem us from wickedness

The third reason is that Jesus *gave himself for us* (verse 14) to save us from our sinful guilt and to set us free (*redeem us*) from all wickedness: 'He died to make us good' wrote Mrs Alexander in her hymn, 'There is a green hill far away'. Transformed beautiful living is the expected result of belief. His finished work achieved our salvation: but the moral force of his death also motivates us to obey him and to become holy. If we continue sinning, we deny the purpose of his dying on our behalf, as though he died in vain.

The glorious future destiny of God's church

But there is still more here (verse 14). The repetition of *us* speaks of Jesus' purpose to redeem us and to *purify for himself a people*, his church (Psalm 130:8; Exodus 19:5, 6; Deuteronomy 7:6; 14:2; 26:18). Words first used of Israel as God's 'treasured possession' are now fulfilled in God's New Covenant people. The final words read, literally, 'zealots for beautiful works'. If we stress Jesus only as a personal Saviour, we may forget that godliness is to be shared by a whole community. It is not clear whether 'you' is singular or plural here: it usually means 'all of us together'. In the New Testament the word 'saint' is always plural, except 'every saint' (Philippians 4:21 NRSV). Our individualism obscures the fact that the Bible expects us to be not a motley crew of patched up sinful individuals, but a whole redeemed community with a lovely corporate lifestyle and a glorious future destiny. Did you ever wonder what human life was all about? Well, this is where we are heading: God's own new redeemed community.

These … things are great foundation truths of the gospel: every church group is to embrace a beautiful holy life full of good deeds.

Questions

1. What reasons are given here for living beautiful lives? How do these truths impact your own lifestyle?
2. List those beliefs and actions which can only be individual and personal to you; and another list which should be shared by the whole fellowship (stop at ten). Which list is longer? Discuss them and make the list again.
3. Given the Cretan character (1:12), and our own current culture, why is the way Christians live so important? How do we rate our success? Is godliness evident?

Does verse 13 explicitly state that Jesus is God?

What does Paul mean here? There is a translation problem. Does he speak of the appearing both of God and of Jesus Christ, two Persons of the Trinity 'appearing'? Or is he stating our Christian belief, that Jesus Christ is God? (i.e., *Lord* as in Romans 10:9; 1 Corinthians 12:3; Philippians 2:11). Liberal scholars dislike this reading of it. However, the single definite article '*the* great God and Saviour' seems to control both nouns, and 'appearing' is never used of God apart from Jesus. It is Jesus who has 'appeared', who gave himself to save us, who will 'appear' the second time and who is our great God and Saviour.

PRACTICAL GOOD WORKS

Titus 3

Titus 3:1–8a

How to achieve a radical change in lifestyle

The new Christian lifestyle should win favour with society as a whole. The Cretans' bad reputation (and their whole lives) are to be transformed by the mercy of God, the power of the Spirit and the gospel of Jesus.

Christian Cretans in the state and society (verses 1–2)

Paul tells Titus to (literally) 'make a regular practice of reminding the people' to obey the authorities. The Cretans were noted for being disorderly, wild and turbulent people, who, understandably, did not like being ruled from Rome. Yet the gospel is able to transform them, even politically, into responsible, law-abiding citizens.

The gospel should change even our cultural traits: the God-given heredity in the new birth is to override our conditioning by a pagan environment. *Peaceable* (verse 2) means 'not pugnacious' (1 Timothy 3:3). The fruit of the Spirit of meekness is to be shown to all human beings whoever they are, whether they are 'family' or not: a very un-Cretan attitude.

What we were like before conversion

Verses 3–7 form the second section of teaching which does not appear in 1 Timothy (see also 2:11–15). A transformed lifestyle is a direct result of the appearing of the *kindness and love* of God our Saviour. We are saved, not because of our own efforts, but through his mercy, the once for all regeneration of baptism and the continual daily renewal of the Holy Spirit poured lavishly upon us. We are already justified by grace and will therefore inherit eternal life. We must be gripped by such truths if we are to live beautiful lives.

Verse 3 provides a devastating description of human society (not just Cretans – *we too*), unregenerate people outside of Christ. This is how the Bible sees humankind before we see the light of the gospel (see Ephesians 2:1–3). *Foolish* literally means 'mindless' for human beings allow themselves actually to be *enslaved by … passions and pleasures*. This darkness of human society shows the need for Christ's light: our dis-grace shows how much we need the grace of God.

The finished work of Christ for us

Verses 4–5a develop what was written in 2:11. The stark contrast with verse 3 is striking, for *kindness and love* are the opposites of *malice* and *hating*. Some people, even some Christians, live in legalistic fear of God as lawgiver and judge and find it hard to accept that God is, indeed, *kind* (see Romans 2:4; 11:22; Ephesians 2:7). Perhaps we think of kindness as uncles giving us sweets, or little girls rescuing chicks or baby rabbits! God's kindness is infinitely more significant and far reaching: his kindness is shown in that he has completed a once for all rescue work in one decisive act on the cross. It is finished! He has done it (Psalm 22:31).

The completed work of the Holy Spirit in us

Paul invites us to remember with gratitude and excitement what the Holy Spirit did for us when we first came to faith (verses 5b–7). It is like stepping beneath a waterfall on a hot day or taking a shower when we are hot and dirty. He speaks of *the washing of rebirth* – here are some pictures of it.

▶ In Israel today you can find many old Jewish ceremonial baths, *miqvot*, used in New Testament times, in front of the temple, at Qumran and synagogues. The person to be cleansed entered 'living' (running) water. The whole body had to be immersed, women even having to remove ribbons from their hair. Such baptism was applied by Jews to Gentile proselytes joining synagogue communities.

▶ In the Song of Songs (4:2; 6:6) the lover describes his lady's teeth as being like sheep that have just come up glistening white out of *the washing*.

▶ The word *rebirth* was used by Jesus when he said 'at the *renewal* of all things, when the Son of Man sits on his glorious throne' (Matthew 19:28).

▶ The same word was used by Stoic philosophers describing the transforming of nature each Spring. As in the old song, 'When my heart was wintry, bleak and full of cold', the quickening work of God causes new life to spring up.

The *washing of rebirth* reminds us of that inward transformation that has already taken place in our lives through the grace of God, portrayed visibly in outward baptism with water.

The continuing work of the Holy Spirit in us

The Church of England's Christmas Day prayer speaks of two stages of the Spirit's work, one complete and the other continuing: 'how that having been made regenerate, we are daily renewed by the Holy Spirit'. *Renewal by the Holy Spirit* is all about the continuing step by step renewing of the Divine image through the daily work of the Holy Spirit within us. We should pause to thank God for the wonder of his spring transforming our bleak wintry lives and to ask him to keep on renewing us by his Holy Spirit day by day. Notice that all three Persons of the Trinity are active. God *poured out* his Holy Spirit *generously through Jesus Christ our Saviour* (verse 6). This started at Pentecost (Acts 2:17, 18; 10:45 quoting Joel 2:28) and has been continuing ever since. There is no danger of the source drying up. Acts 2:33 sees Jesus doing the pouring; 'He has received from the Father the promised Holy Spirit and poured out what you now see and hear'.

We have been *justified by his grace* (verse 7); Paul uses here the same language of the law courts as does Romans 3:24; 8:33. This is nicely expressed in pidgin English as 'God 'e say I'm alright'! Through the kindness, mercy and grace of God we are now regarded as righteous, but there is more. We have become his children through rebirth, and therefore also his *heirs*, inheriting the sure and certain *hope of eternal life*.

What is the *trustworthy saying* (verse 8)? It seems to point back to this reliable and concise explanation of the central core of the gospel. If we were trying to write a creed it would be difficult to produce anything more concise than this, no telegram could use fewer words! Four verses have reminded us of:

Incarnation (verse 4)
Calvary (verse 5)
Pentecost (verse 6)
Heaven (verse 7)
Justification (verse 7)
New birth (verse 5)
Sanctification (verse 5)
Future inheritance (verse 7).

This is likely to be an early creed or statement of faith.

Questions

---

1. Look again at verses 5 and 6 and the pictures of washing described on p. 156. Think of more images of cleansing that appeal to you. How do they mirror the feelings of your own new birth?
2. Discuss and agree the wording for an eight point creed or basic summary of the faith as suggested above. Is there anything you would not have included? Has anything vital been missed out?
3. In the larger context of this whole letter to Titus, should Christians obey the state authorities? What exceptions might there be? Why?

Titus 3:8b–15

Parting instructions

Paul continues to stress a beautiful lifestyle avoiding quarrels and religious arguments, along with some practical instructions.

A transformed and beautiful lifestyle (verse 8) is the major emphasis of this letter, returned to yet again in verse 14. Whatever the Cretans were like before they must be different now.
Again and again Paul stresses the importance of Cretan Christians giving visible evidence of their genuine conversion by beautiful living (see *Good Works*, p. 162).

Warnings about divisiveness and argumentativeness

False teaching was such a menace in these young congregations that Paul comes back to it at the end of his letter (verses 9–11). The warnings were more urgent in 1 Timothy 1:4 and 6:4 but the ideas are the same. Bad news may travel as fast as good news: false teaching spreads as fast as the gospel, so stamp it out! To cause division in a fellowship is both stupid and sinful.

▶ The emphatic word *foolish* (verse 9) translates the word from which we derive 'moronic'. Windy arguments are stupid; they distract Christian workers, who really have no time to waste on such idiocy.

▶ *Divisive person* (verse 10) is a phrase used uniquely here in the New Testament. Luke uses the related Greek noun when referring to Sadducees (Acts 5:17); Pharisees (Acts 15:5); and Christians (Acts 24:5). Paul uses it of partisan cliques (1 Corinthians 11:19; Galatians 5:20).

▶ *Have nothing to do with him* (verse 10) probably means 'to leave out of account, ignore' rather than formally put out of the church. Such people are to be given two warnings: only on the third occasion is there to be rejection.

▶ *Warped and sinful* (verse 11) are equally strong words. Such divisive people are not just silly, but sinful in the sight of God. People like this are a menace, especially in a small independent church where one person can bring a whole congregation into bondage to his or her own fads and legalisms. Christians need to see that to disrupt the church is a terrible sin (1 Corinthians 3:17).

Closing instructions and greetings

We switch now from warnings about awkward people to detailed and practical instructions about real places and real people (verse 12). We get more important clues about the timing and occasion of the letter from these closing verses than from anywhere else.

Where was *Nicopolis* and why should Paul spend the winter there? It means 'Victory town', named after the victory of Augustus over Anthony and Cleopatra in 31 BC at Actium, and was on the Adriatic coast of Greece. Ships were brought ashore in the autumn and laid up for the winter (the storms were too much for them), so sea travel came to a virtual standstill. Overland journeys became hazardous too, especially over mountain passes choked with snow. Thus an experienced traveller like Paul would look for a winter haven to hole up in until transport was available again in the spring. Nicopolis would be a good launching place for Titus to continue up the coast to Dalmatia (2 Timothy 4:10).

Paul did not want Titus to leave until either *Artemas or Tychichus* came to replace him even though local elders had been appointed. Paul seems to feel that the Cretans still need to be supervised. (Those who are curious about Tychichus should refer to Acts 20:4; Ephesians 6:21; Colossians 4:7 and 2 Timothy 4:12).

Who were *Zenas* and *Apollos*? Perhaps they were carrying the letter to Titus. We know nothing else of Zenas. Apollos was the gifted Jewish evangelist, befriended by Aquila and Priscilla (Acts 18:24–28) and mentioned in 1 Corinthians 1:12, who came from Alexandria. Luke is silent in Acts about the evangelization of Alexandria, the second largest city of the Roman empire, next only to Rome and larger than Antioch. Apollos may well have evangelized it. Hospitality among Christians was very much a feature of the early church.

Even in the middle of sending personal greetings and a request for hospitality for the travellers, Paul returns to the theme that has dominated the letter: *Our people must learn to devote themselves to doing what is good … and not to live unproductive lives.* Paul's vision is that Christian communities by their beautiful way of living (even in Crete) will commend the gospel to all.

The final *Grace be with you all* points to the fact that this letter, although addressed to Titus, was intended to be read by all the new Christians in Crete.

Questions

1. How can we recapture Paul's urgency to see transformed lives in our churches? How can this transformation happen?
2. We are saved by God's grace, so why are 'good works' so important to us as individuals and as fellowships of believers?
3. Are splits and divisions a feature of your church life? How can these be tackled in the light of Paul's letter to Titus? Warning: you will need care and sensitivity if you tackle this question.

Titus the enthusiast

If Joseph of Cyprus so displayed the gift of 'encouragement' that he was nicknamed Barnabas, 'son of encouragement' or 'son of prophecy' (Acts 4:36), one wonders whether Titus also might have earned a nickname. Four times in 2 Corinthians 8:16–24 the same Greek root word occurs in describing Titus, translated variously as 'concern' (verse 16), 'enthusiasm' (verse 17) and 'zealous' and 'confidence' (verse 22). Paul actually uses the related verb about Titus in 3:12 when he says 'hasten' or 'hurry' to Nicopolis, and the adverb in 3:13, *Diligently help Zenas and Apollos*, almost as though Paul was gently teasing Titus for all his enthusiasm and keenness. The basic idea is that of 'eagerness' or 'diligence'.

This gives us an attractive picture of this eager Greek, whose fellowship meant so much to Paul. Paul says, 'I still had no peace of mind, because I did not find my brother Titus there', waiting for him in Troas with news of Corinth (2 Corinthians

2:13). Then after a long digression we read, 'God who comforts the depressed, comforted us by the coming of Titus' (2 Corinthians 7:6). What a lovely thing to say of any fellow-Christian. Later he says, 'Titus has the same eagerness I have' (2 Corinthians 8:16) and 'he is coming to you with much enthusiasm and on his own initiative' (2 Corinthians 8:17). Alford comments, 'He was too eager to need any exhortations!' What excellent qualities these are in a missionary colleague.

'Good works' in Paul's letter to Titus

It is sometimes said that Paul has no time for good works and is concerned only for faith. James, we are told, is the 'good works man'. But it would be hard to find a stronger emphasis on good works in the letter to Titus, even in James.

- ▶ *Unfit for doing anything good* (1:16) describes the rebellious people.

- ▶ *Eager to do what is good* (2:14). God's purpose is that we should be 'zealots' (eager) for good works.

- ▶ *Ready to do whatever is good* (3:1) in the context of the state and society.

- ▶ *Devote themselves to doing what is good* (3:8), that is, 'beautiful works'.

- ▶ *Learn to devote themselves to doing what is good* (3:14) as a parting shot.

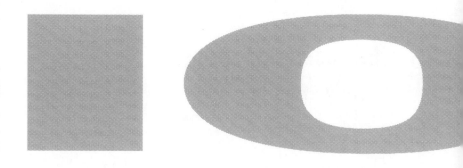

DON'T BE ASHAMED

2 Timothy 1

Introduction to 2 Timothy

Paul's situation

This third Pastoral letter, similar to the other two in language and style, has a different purpose. Paul, in addressing his agents-in-place in Ephesus and Crete in 1 Timothy and Titus, expected that the local church would read those letters over their shoulders. This, however, is a truly personal letter asking Timothy to leave Ephesus to join Paul in Rome in the final crisis of his life. The first letter says *stay* in Ephesus, and the second letter says *leave*.

Paul has been arrested again and is back in prison in Rome (1:16–17; 2:9). He has had a preliminary trial (4:16–17) and expects to be sentenced to death (4:6–7). Now he wants to pass over his mantle to Timothy. Only Luke is with him, suggesting that Luke may have acted as Paul's secretary for all three letters. As we understand Paul's situation the more we are moved by this last testament – like Moses handing over to Joshua (Deuteronomy 31:7–8), or Elijah to Elisha (2 Kings 2:6–15).

This letter is not just an interesting piece of first-century Greek literature: it speaks to our hearts, calling us to similar commitment to Christ. It demands a response from us. Don't potter! Don't fritter away your life in ways that do not build the Kingdom. Be committed as Paul was and as he urges Timothy to be. Paul is faithful to the death after a lifetime of costly sacrifice. He keeps right on to the end of the road.

2 Timothy 1:1–5

Greetings from death row

Even with a sentence of death hanging over him Paul give thanks for Timothy's faithful life.

 Paul uses a standard, simple address which differs from his first letter to Timothy only in the significant phrase *according to the promise of life that is in Christ Jesus*. Paul, with the prospect of a death sentence in the forefront of his mind, is trusting the promise of life made by the Lord Jesus (John 5:21; 6:54). Christ Jesus, the Living One, also executed by the Romans, was dead but is alive again. He has the keys of death and Hades, to deliver Paul (and us) from and through death. This doctrine strengthens Paul in adversity. *'True son in the faith'* (1 Timothy 1:2) is replaced by *my dear son* (verse 2), a warm address forming the basis of his appeal to Timothy throughout the letter.

Verses 3–5 are one long sentence in the original Greek. Ancient letter writing convention (brushed aside in Galatians and 1 Timothy because Paul wants to get down to business and deal urgently with error), followed opening thanks with prayer for the person addressed, as in Philippians 1:3–11 and Colossians 1:3–11.

Paul thanks God for his colleague

In thanking God for Timothy, Paul recognizes all that Timothy has become as a result of God's work in him. They are both indebted to their Jewish heritage. Note the parallel between Paul's 'forefathers' (verse 3) and Timothy's mother and grandmother (verse 5), his 'foremothers' if you like. Both men may rejoice in their Jewish roots, in contrast with false teachers, untrue to their past, who misuse the Old Testament. We know that our family of origin does much to shape our lives. Onesiphorus (verse 16) also relates to his *household*. Paul thanks God for Lois and Eunice's *sincere* (genuine) *faith* (cf. 1 Timothy 1:5). Calvin comments that Timothy 'was reared in his infancy in such a way that he could suck in godliness along with his mother's milk'. His mother and grandmother had such a genuine faith, and so does Timothy himself. Paul now appeals to Timothy, on the basis of this true commitment.

Paul, the man of integrity

Paul's situation is desperate: *his prisoner . . . suffering for the gospel* (verse 8); *suffering as I am* (verse 12); *my chains* (verse 16); *suffering . . . to the point of being chained like a criminal* (2:9). Though he has been thrown into prison like a criminal, Paul has a clear or 'purified conscience' (see 1 Timothy 1:5 and contrast with the 'seared' or 'cauterized consciences' of the false teachers in 1 Timothy 4:2). Such integrity of conscience is essential for every Christian worker, but not everyone has it. A clear conscience, once lost, is difficult to retrieve: so we must by all means keep it clean.

Paul, the man of prayer

Paul prayed for people he knew by name: *night and day . . . constantly* (verse 3) does not mean continuously, but regularly (as in Acts 20:31 when Paul was admonishing the Ephesians night and day for three years). In this letter Paul mentions no fewer than twenty-two people by name, almost as many as in Romans 16. The practice of listing the people you meet and praying for them is a good one: that way you never forget people or their names, and they become your friends.

Paul, the man who values Christian friendship

Recalling their last tearful farewell is a warm, emotional aside in the middle of the sentence (verse 4: compare Acts 20:37), and already introduces the main purpose of the letter: 'I long to see you'. Paul wants Timothy to join him in Rome before the end comes: 'Come quickly' (4:9) and 'Come before winter' (4:21). *I have been reminded* (verse 5) or 'having received a reminder of' suggests that Paul has just received a letter or news about Timothy.

Questions

1. Do you have godly relatives or spiritual mentors as Timothy did? Then make a list or share some stories about what they have done for you, thanking the Lord for them.
2. We are not meant to live a solitary Christian life, but rather the church is meant to supply us with a network or web of relationships: in what ways are we helping one another to build such bonding relationships into our own congregation? How can we do better?
3. Since our 'roots' exercise such a strong influence on us, is it reasonable to expect anyone to change (e.g., from Islam to Christianity, from atheist to believer)? Share some examples and discuss the problems.

2 Timothy 1:6-7

Fan into flame the Spirit's gifts

The 'charismata', or grace-gifts from God, are meant to be used, and need to be cultivated.

Timothy has had the privilege of a godly upbringing and, on top of that blessing, God has gifted him with special gifts or 'graces' to be used in the service of the churches. But  these gifts do not work automatically. We need to use them if they are to do what God desires. A box of matches has the potential to produce a massive blaze, but even matches need to be struck.

God's gift is in you

Timothy must therefore fan into flame the 'charisma' he has from God, knowing that the Holy Spirit, who lives in us, does not make us timid, but gives us power, love and discipline (verses 6–7). *For this reason*, that is, because of the genuine faith Timothy has, *I remind you to fan into flame the gift of God* (compare 1 Timothy 4:14: 'do not neglect your gift').

Just possessing a gift is not enough unless it is used and cultivated through diligent effort. He must 'stir up that inner fire': the small glowing ember must be fanned into a roaring blaze. So let your gifts burn for the Lord, my brothers and sisters

168

(Paul used the same picture in the first of all his letters, 1 Thessalonians 5:19: 'Do not put out the Spirit's fire').

Which is in you through the laying on of my hands. In his first letter Paul reminded Timothy of the laying on of hands by the whole body of elders at Lystra (1 Timothy 4:14), but in this personal letter, Paul reminds Timothy of when he himself had laid hands on him when he first joined Paul and Silas. We should not read back modern notions of clerical status or 'priestly ordination' into the text. The New Testament knows no such distinctions between 'clergy' and 'lay people': all Christian workers need to be recognized by the churches which appoint them. God's spirit is in you all.

Verse 7 begins with a negative: 'No way did God give us a timid Spirit'. The Holy Spirit with a capital 'S' (as in verse 14), is meant and not our human 'spirit' with a small 's'. Because Christ lives in us through his Spirit, we should be characterized not by timid embarassment, but by 'power and love and a sound mind'. That is, not cowardly fear, but God's strength, his love for people and that sanity and self-control so much admired by the Greeks.

If Paul is in prison and Nero is running amok, then most Christians would timidly lie low and say nothing. Ancient tradition tells us that both Peter and Paul met their deaths in Nero's persecution. It seems there was some panic and loss of morale among local Christians (verse 15). Who can blame them: would a Russian willingly have visited someone held by the KGB in Lubyanka prison?

Questions

1. Make a list, however long or short, of the gifts God has given you. Which needs fanning into flame? How will you do it?
2. In your group, make a list of *each other's* gifts as you see them. Share your lists and prepare for some surprises. Then pray for one another.

3. Is there a difference between the gifts of the Spirit and the indwelling of the Spirit himself? How would you describe the difference? Is one more important than the other?

2 Timothy 1:8–11

Timothy is not to be ashamed

How can we be ashamed of the glorious inheritance which God has given to us?

The key words of this chapter are 'not ashamed'. They occur in verses 8 (twice), 12 and 16. Timothy is not to be ashamed of testifying, of suffering or of Paul. Paul is 'not ashamed' (verse 12) and neither is Onesiphorus (verse 16).

So do not be ashamed to testify about our Lord (verse 8). Paul perhaps recalls the words of Jesus in Luke 9:26 (which Luke, working on his gospel, would already know). After all 'our Lord' Jesus had been crucified as an evildoer by the Romans. You took a risk if you sided with him in public when persecution was raging. *Or ashamed of me his prisoner*. Paul is now a state prisoner, soon to be condemned. Being a Roman citizen he would be beheaded with a sword, rather than crucified on a cross as Peter was. *But* (rather than being ashamed) *join with me in suffering for the gospel*. Paul coins a word here meaning 'suffer evil together with'.

The early Christians were not supermen: nobody likes suffering. It is only possible *by the power of God*. Paul reminds suffering saints that God's power is there on tap to make us bold. Are we tempted to be timid? The early church prayed for boldness (Acts 4:29) and their prayers were answered (Acts 4:31).

We are saved to serve

As he so often does, Paul launches into a great statement about God (verse 9). He may be quoting an early Christian hymn or catechism, enriching his own thoughts: *Who has saved us and called us to a holy life* (calling). Being saved is only a part of what God plans for us: he also calls us to serve. We cannot be content to be saved without accepting responsibility to work for his cause. Repetition of 'called' (not in the NIV) always points to living in the church: to live a life worthy of belonging to God's church (Ephesians 4:1).

Not because of anything we have done, but because of his own purpose and grace is a lovely statement of God's grace taking the initiative in our salvation (see Titus 3:5); *but it has now been revealed through the appearing of our Saviour Christ Jesus* (verse 10) that is, in his incarnation (see Titus 2:11) *who has destroyed death and brought life and immortality to light through the gospel.* The apostle, awaiting execution, rejoices at the prospect of 'life and immortality'. Timid Timothy needs reminding of it too: the Romans are most efficient at killing the body, but can do no more!

That is why Christians can share in suffering, because we know the gospel is about overcoming death and mortality. The resurrection of the body, which we confess in the creeds, is a basic Christian belief. Nothing less will fortify Christians suffering persecution and martyrdom. Pause here to pray for fellow Christians, who even now may be suffering for their faith somewhere in the world.

Paul has been appointed as herald, apostle and teacher

The words suggest three succeeding roles: first, a royal herald proclaims the Good News of the Kingdom to people who have never heard it before – the evangelist's role; second, the apostle plants churches; third, the teacher trains new disciples to obey

Christ. This was Paul's calling and these were the spiritual gifts which qualified him to be a missionary to the nations. The word 'missionary' has been debased to mean an odd-job man filling odd vacancies abroad! We must return to this biblical understanding of what a missionary does, as is shown in the Books of Acts. It is precisely because of this calling (if Paul had remained a Jewish rabbi in Jerusalem this would never have happened), *that is why I am suffering as I am.*

Questions

1. Why is it so hard to talk about Jesus to unbelievers? How can we find help with this problem?
2. How does assurance about our future resurrection help us to put up with suffering? How do we answer those who accuse us of believing in 'pie in the sky when you die'?
3. What place is there for 'missionaries' in the modern world? Which countries need them?

2 Timothy 1:12–14

Paul is not ashamed

It is no cause for shame to suffer for the Lord's sake.

Yet I am not ashamed (verse 12) and so I am an example to you, Timothy. That is, though Paul is in gaol as an evildoer in the view of his captors, he knows he is suffering for Christ's cause and so feels no shame in being in prison. Paul knows in whom he has trusted and his confidence is in a Lord who was also arrested and led off by soldiers, mocked, tortured and put to death and who rose again. Paul has entrusted his own life and eternal destiny into the hands of his Lord, who will guard what has been deposited with him.

Although the NIV introduces a paragraph break after verse 12 the sense continues. *Keep as the pattern* means having this example, the same word as 1 Timothy 1:16 for a model, an outline sketch or a rough draft. 'Of the healthy words you heard from me', with faith and love in Christ Jesus. From Paul Timothy has a model of teaching, but from Christ he has faith and love. While Timothy is committed to the outline of teaching he has received from Paul, in Christ he has freedom to develop it in the living circumstances of the street. Paul's theology is not abstract theory studied in the library, but practical, worked out in the street as he meets concrete problems in troubled churches. We too need to make our theology real as we witness and debate with unchurched people, and use the Scriptures to do it.

Guard the good deposit that was entrusted to you is the splendid trust of the unchanging gospel which Paul has deposited with Timothy for safekeeping (see comment on 1 Timothy 6:20). But how can this timid man hope to hold it safe? *With the help of the Holy Spirit who lives in us.* So this section ends, as it began (verse 7), with a reminder of the work of the Holy Spirit within us, making us bold and faithful even when the going is tough: the passage hangs together.

Questions

1. In essence what is the 'good deposit' of 'sound teaching'? Can you summarize the gospel as if for an unbeliever?
2. What resources are available to Christians walking with the Holy Spirit (compare Luke 12:11–12)? Share some examples of how he has provided help.
3. Does this passage apply differently to naturally timid people and to naturally bold? Why? Why not?

2 Timothy 1:15–18

Onesiphorus is not ashamed

**We read examples of some who failed
to be faithful and one who succeeded.**

In Paul's miserable situation, feeling that *everyone* in (or from) Asia had deserted him, only Onesiphorus from Ephesus was 'not ashamed' of Paul's chains.

The last four verses of chapter 1 speak of Asians who failed and only one who gloriously succeeded. Paul can hardly mean that everyone in Asia (a Roman province in present-day Turkey) has deserted him (when Timothy is there still and Paul is in Rome). That would be a wild exaggeration. But rather, *You know that everyone from the province of Asia has deserted me, including Phygelus and Hermogenes,* that is, it is not people *in* Asia, but people *from* Asia in Rome, who were not prepared to risk visiting Paul in prison. This need not mean that they had rejected the gospel, but rather, that it was too risky or shameful to associate with Paul as a Christian leader about to be sentenced. The same forlorn feeling of being betrayed and forsaken is expressed in 2 Timothy 4:16. Paul was not complaining, but he could not help expressing his feelings of sadness and isolation.

Refreshment from Onesiphorus

Some think Onesiphorus may already have died because of the reference to *the household of Onesiphorus*, but the words need mean no more than that his household was in Ephesus, while the man himself was in Rome. His name means 'A bringer of profit' (as Christopher means a bearer of Christ) and is related to the name Onesimus, the converted slave of Philemon 11 who now lives up to his name of being 'profitable'. Paul asks for present mercy for the household and future mercy in the Day of Judgment (verse 18) for Onesiphorus himself.

Because he often refreshed me (verse 16). Those in prison, (as in hospitals in Asia still) were required to provide their own food. The verb 'refresh' occurs only here in the New Testament, though a related noun occurs in Acts 3:19, 'times of refreshing', of blessing for the church. *And was not ashamed of my chains.* Even though consorting with someone under sentence of death might make him suspect, this man visited and refreshed the apostle again and again. So, far from being ashamed or afraid when he came to Rome *he searched diligently for me until he found me.* Paul may not have been in one of the normal public prisons, for the impression is that he was not easily found.

So unlike many who have deserted me, dear Timothy, you follow the example of this good man who was not ashamed (verse 16) of witnessing to the gospel or of me, God's prisoner. Paul is hurting: some who had confessed Christ, were now compromising and falling away. God forbid that this happen to Timothy: may he not be ashamed, and be willing to visit Paul in death row. *May the Lord grant that he* (who took such trouble to *find* him – Paul is playing with words again) *will find mercy from the Lord on that day*, the final day of judgment. This may shock Protestants, as it could be a unique prayer for someone who is dead, though it amounts only to commending him to the Divine mercy. But then, of course, Timothy will recall *in how many ways he helped me in Ephesus.* So Onesiphorus had served in Ephesus in the past. These are vivid cameos of individuals. Can we believe that such details have been invented about the fictional visits of a make-believe character to give credibility to a letter written long after Paul was dead, as liberal scholars allege?

Questions

1. Do you feel sometimes that 'everyone' has deserted you and circumstances are all stacked up against you? Take time to talk to God about it and try to see yourself from his point of view.
2. Onesiphorus took visiting seriously. How far is it the task of all Christians to visit the sick, elderly, imprisoned and foreigners? Work out together in your group how the time can be found (compare Matthew 25:36, 43; James 1:27 AV).
3. Is there any point in praying for those who have died? Why? Why not?

WORKING IN
GOD'S STRENGTH

2 Timothy 2

2 Timothy 2:1–2

Teaching gifts are to be shared

Timothy is to be strong in the grace-gift of teaching, passing on what he has heard to others, both men and women, who can teach others in turn.

How is Timothy strong?

Be strong. The command in this context differs both from similar commands to Joshua to fight (Joshua 1:6–7) and to the Ephesian warrior church (Ephesians 6:10) to battle by means of prayer. Where does this strength come from? It is *the grace that is in Christ Jesus*. This strength comes from the Lord. It is not the power that comes from natural bounce, strong personality or sheer physical energy: but from God's grace. But for what purpose is this grace available to Timothy: in exercising what gift of grace is Timothy to be strong?

Timothy's gift is clear in the context of the whole chapter: he is to entrust what he himself has been taught to reliable people (verse 2), he must correctly handle the word of truth (verse 15), and he must be able to teach. He must gently instruct (verses 24 and 25). In other words, this verse means: 'Timothy is to be strong in the ability given to him by Christ for teaching'. What is he to teach? *The things you have heard me say*. The tense implies not, on one occasion, but rather the total sum of all the truth that

Timothy has soaked up from Paul over many years: this 'deposit' must be passed on intact to others. For us today this truth is all God has revealed in the whole Bible.

Who is Timothy to teach?

Entrust to reliable who? Both the NIV and AV say 'men', which might be mistaken for 'males'. Paul uses an inclusive Greek word that usually means 'human beings' of either gender (though it can sometimes refer to males, as in 1 Corinthians 7:1; Matthew 19:5 and Ephesians 5:31, quoting Genesis 2:24) (see p. 58 on 1 Timothy 2:12). If ever the apostle intended (as sadly, some people still try to assert from 1 Timothy 2:12) to ban any woman from teaching on any subject at any time, then he had a great opportunity to do it here by using the clear, exclusive word for 'males': and – he does not. Comparing Scripture with Scripture means that a plain, simple verse in a straightforward context like 2 Timothy 2:2 decides how we interpret 1 Timothy 2:12 (which is a difficult verse in a difficult context). In Philippians 4:3 Paul calls women 'colleagues' (fellow-workers) and members of the same team (fellow-athletes), while in Romans 16 he commends the ministry of seven women. All men who have served abroad as missionaries respect, honour and commend the women who have laboured alongside them as fellow-workers.

How is the succession to be ensured?

Whether we are male or female, it is not enough to have been taught the truth, we must pass it on to others: Paul to Timothy; Timothy to faithful persons; faithful men and women to others. As in the four laps of a relay race, each person must pass on what they have learned to the next runner. How stupid is the Christian leader who insists on trying to do it all solo! The secret of being an effective missionary like Paul is that you are always training up others to continue and expand the work. We are not just to serve up cakes, or even teach recipes, but to train master bakers, who will train more master bakers! This is the simple secret of church growth: train more and more workers and let them loose! Paul's present circumstances, when leaders may be arrested and executed, lend all the greater urgency to training up successors.

Questions

———————————————

1. Are you in a position to pass on your gifts and insights to others? How can you best encourage others to use their gifts?
2. Do you detect any preference in your church for men (or women?) for certain jobs? Are there male and female roles or should all be open to everyone?
3. Selfish one-man-band style leadership fetters fellow believers in the pews as a captive, passive audience. What does this passage suggest enlightened biblical leadership should do? Is such biblical policy only applicable in pioneer situations?

2 Timothy 2:3–7

Understanding hardship

———————————————

Salvation is by God's grace, but the Christian is called to a life of extremely hard work.

Paul writes, *Reflect on what I am saying, and the Lord will give you insight into all this* (verse 7). Paul gives us three pictures to help us understand why the Christian life is sometimes so tough. Why does he choose soldiers, athletes and farmers?

▶ All are people who sweat and work hard.

▶ All three pass on what they have learned to others: drill sergeants to recruits; coaches to athletes and farmers to their sons.

▶ All see results only if they persevere over an extended period of time.

▶ They are goal-orientated people who are motivated by clear purposes.

The three pictures resemble each other in these four respects, but differ in other ways.

The soldier (verses 3–4): without sacrifices there are no victories

The soldier in Paul's day lives simply, and puts up with hardship, because he has a single-minded sense of purpose. He therefore remains detached from civilian entanglements and family ties that would weaken his commitment to his priorities. His desire is to please the officer who leads him. What lesson does Paul draw? Making sacrifices is essential to being a good soldier.

For 1800 years the international enterprise of pioneering the gospel was spearheaded mainly by celibate men (and a few women). Until the widespread availability of birth control in the early twentieth century, married people tended to have a baby every couple of years or less; for example, Maria Hudson Taylor, wife of the founder of the China Inland Mission, had eight babies in eleven years. No way could Paul have walked 30 miles a day, with one child on his shoulders, leading another by the hand, while his wife led a couple more! Peter may have been accompanied by his wife, but they were older and the children left behind. Celibacy was a necessary condition for missionaries then (see 1 Corinthians 7:8).

Jesus Christ is the leader whom we seek to please. Because a soldier knows that his life may be short he has a sense of urgency to get things done while there is time. The seventeenth-century puritan Richard Baxter, who suffered from poor health, is said to have preached every sermon as though it was his last, as somebody who was dying, to others who were also on their way to death. The stress here is on enduring hardship (see verses 3, 9, 10, 12).

The athlete (verse 5): without discipline there are no prizes

The athlete schools himself, training hard, because he wants to win. The classical writer Pausanias tells us that athletes entering for the Olympic Games had to swear before a statue of Zeus that they had trained for ten months beforehand: there could be no decision to run at the last moment. So to run *according to the rules* or, 'lawfully', requires months of hard training. The training of gymnasts, skaters, footballers or any athletes demands constant practice and strict discipline if you want results. A recent book by Patrick McElligott shows how, though leaving school with minimal education, he worked at learning the Japanese language: an O-level, A-level, BA and finally PhD. That kind of sweat and discipline to fit oneself for ministry illustrates what Paul is getting at.

The farmer (verse 6): without sweat there is no harvest

The farmer works hard, all through the year, year after year, so that he may enjoy his share of the crops. Farming demands unremitting toil to the point of exhaustion. There are no pauses: as soon as one hardworking year is over, a new year of hard work begins. *Hardworking* is a technical word Paul uses also for ministerial labour. A missionary told me it took an average of twenty visits to a Japanese home before anyone came to church and an average of one hundred visits before anyone came to faith and baptism. Christian workers must be committed to work hard in season and out of season, studying hard and preparing thoroughly in order to reap a harvest.

Reflect on what I am saying, for the Lord will give you insight into all this. Verse 7 reminds us that we must use the minds God gave us to think and puzzle out the truths of Scripture. At the same time it shows us that it is the Lord, through his Holy Spirit who enlightens and illuminates our minds to understand the true meaning of a passage from the Bible. We do not have to choose between being intellectual or being spiritual: we must love the Lord with heart *and* mind. I must not be content with barren intellectualism on the one hand, or an anti-intellectual following of subjective whimsies on the other. We must love the Lord with all our minds: and use the minds he has given us for his glory. We must study what a passage really means, illumined by the Spirit and then apply it to daily life, inspired by the Spirit. God promises to illumine those who think! Christians are always looking for an easy way and 'instant' methods: there is no encouragement here for a spiritual 'get out'.

Questions

1. Do you think of yourself as a soldier, an athlete or a farmer in Christian terms? What can you learn from each comparison?
2. What is the 'grace' in which Timothy is to be strong, and for what purpose has it been given to him (verses 2, 15, 24, 25)? Is your church a good teaching church? How can it be improved?
3. How can Paul's call to hard work be reconciled with the old call to 'let go and let God' and the newer advice 'do not strive'?

2 Timothy 2:8–13

Paul's example of sufferings

Paul is not urging Timothy to a life he himself does not live: his own life is an example of suffering hardship.

Paul himself is back in prison because he too has been single-minded. He has more to offer Timothy than words; 'the things you have heard me say'. He himself is an outstanding example of the Christian soldier, athlete and hardworking farmer in 'the things you have seen me do'. His lonely, celibate and hardworking life shows his refusal to get entangled with home comforts.

Remember Jesus Christ, raised from the dead, descended from David. This is my gospel (verse 8). What is Paul's train of thought here? Jesus, the anointed Messiah, suffered rejection and the cross while his ancestor David, though anointed king, was a refugee relentlessly pursued by Saul. Timothy will remember that both Jesus and David knew what it was to endure hardships and sufferings, and yet they triumphed over them all. In Romans 1:3–4 the mention of David reminds us of the humanity of Jesus, who can therefore, also suffer and die. But the fact that Christ is risen reminds us as well of his divinity and victory over death.

For which I am suffering even to the point of being chained like a criminal (verse 9). Paul's first imprisonment in Rome was in his own hired house, but this seems more unpleasant: chained like a felon (a word used of the robbers crucified with Jesus) even though he was an innocent Roman citizen. But even if the apostle is chained up, God's Word is not! If, like Paul, you expect to have your life ended soon what do you care most about? That God's Word will go on being proclaimed, taught and taken to the ends of the earth, whatever the cost to yourself and other human lives? Paul cares more about the gospel of God's word than anything else: 'guard the good deposit' (1:14); 'the things you have heard me say ... entrust to reliable persons' (2:2); correctly handle the word of truth (2:15). The prospect of death always clarifies the mind! *Therefore I endure everything for the sake of the elect, that they too may obtain the salvation that is in Christ Jesus, with eternal glory* (verse 10). Paul endures and suffers so that the church may be built up.

Paul knows there is no progress without pain; no birth without travail. In Paul's thinking the suffering of the saints, while not redemptive like the suffering of Jesus, is for 'the sake of the body' (see Colossians 1:24). All that Paul is going through is worth it if it achieves its object – the victory for which the soldier fights, the trophy for which athletes train, the harvest for which farmers sweat: namely that people may be saved through Christ Jesus and enter his glory. Paul's own commitment marvellously illustrates his three pictures.

Another 'trustworthy saying'

The fifth (and final) trustworthy saying (see p. 41) seems to be four lines from a hymn or poem well known by the early church and Timothy, and perfectly fits this context of suffering (verse 9):

► *If we died with him, we will also live with him.* While this may have meant 'die in baptism', it points also to Paul's expected death, and equally expected resurrection with Jesus Christ.

▶ *If we endure, we will also reign with him.* This is relevant to Paul, and to Timothy who both 'endure'.

▶ *If we disown him, he will also disown us.* These solemn words echo Matthew 10:33 and warn us of the results of deliberate turning away from God, but they are followed at once by the reminder that God is more faithful than we are.

▶ *If we are faithless, he will remain faithful, for he cannot disown himself.* No way does God keep his promises to us only if we keep our promises to him. That is unthinkable. We are secure, because he is utterly faithful and reliable. Here is the theological basis for earlier encouragement to Timothy: *God did not give us the spirit of timidity . . . so do not be ashamed to testify about our Lord, or ashamed of me his prisoner. But join with me in suffering for the gospel* (1:7–8). He does not give up on us when we fail or make a mess of things. Hebrews 13:23 tells of Timothy being released from prison, so we know that he did suffer as his mentor did, though we do not know whether it was before or after Paul's death.

Questions

1. What sufferings have you encountered on Christ's behalf? Have they helped you? Anybody else? Brought glory to God?
2. How would the words of this hymn help someone wavering in their commitment to Christ in the face of persecution?
3. How far will the world respect Christianity through its success? How far through its sufferings? Was Jesus Christ successful?

2 Timothy 2:14–19

Sensitive Christianity 1:
Sensitive to Scripture

Hard work by itself and readiness to suffer hardship alone do not equip Christian workers to cope sensitively with troubled church situations. Christian work requires sensitivity and reflection, and not just activism.

Note that Paul is writing against a background of false teaching and division (see verses 14, 18 and 23). He provides three more pictures of how Timothy may cope with this situation.

Good workers

Do your best to present yourself to God, as one approved, a workman who does not need to be ashamed and correctly handles the word of truth (verse 15). Paul repeats the phrase *not . . . ashamed* which we met four times in chapter 1, referring to himself, Timothy and Onesiphorus. A worker should be ashamed of shoddy and incompetent work. The word 'workman' occurs sixteen times in the New Testament. Here it seems to refer to labourers who make roads, because the word translated as *correctly handles* ('rightly divides' AV) means literally 'cut straight'. It refers to cutting roads in the only two other places it is used in Scripture: 'He will make your paths straight' (Proverbs 3:6); 'The righteousness of the blameless makes a straight way for them' (Proverbs 11:5).

Roman roads were proverbially straight ones, and Paul had walked a lot of them! Timothy, in his teaching of the word of truth, is to be like a road maker who cuts straight paths through it. This is Paul's fourth illustration in this chapter (see p. 180). The dramatist Sophocles used the same word for 'to expound soundly'. If Timothy is to confront false teaching he must study Scripture carefully and understand it properly, and not in any sloppy, careless, cavalier way. He must work diligently at his teaching. And all of us must listen carefully and critically to what we hear said and taught, and test it alongside Scripture.

Bad workers

There is a deliberate contrast here with bad workmen like the false teachers Hymenaeus and Philetus (verses 17, 18) 'who have swerved from the truth', deviating from the straight road of teaching. The sorcerer Elymas was told off for 'making crooked the straight paths of the Lord' (Acts 13:10: Amplified Bible). Paul rebuked Peter and others for 'not walking in line with the truth of the gospel' (Galatians 2:14). Sound teaching requires hard study and preparation to cut a straight, accurate road. Lazy Christians who misuse Scripture through shoddy preparation hinder the progress of the gospel.

Avoid godless chatter, because those who indulge in it will become more and more ungodly (verse 16). There are unapproved workmen, who (literally) 'will advance', perhaps a slogan of the false teachers, who will indeed make progress (ironically), but in the wrong direction towards ungodliness! Paul has a gift with words.

Their teaching will spread like gangrene (verse 17). Paul uses a medical picture here (see *Sound/Healthy* p. 148). The effect of false teaching is the opposite of 'healthy words'. False sects spread so quickly – like gangrene! Hymenaeus was mentioned in the first letter (1 Timothy 1:20) as one of the two teachers in Ephesus whom Paul put out of the church. He is still living in the province as a thorn in the side of the Ephesian church.

They say that the resurrection has already taken place, and they destroy the faith of some (verse 18). Some people, both then and today, try to 'spiritualize' the resurrection of believers as present experience, rather than a future physical reality. Paul, under sentence of death, knows that his only hope is Jesus Christ, risen from the dead, who will raise him up also. Leprosy patients with fingers, toes and noses rotted off also want a real physical resurrection. Heresy about the resurrection is as old as this chapter (and 1 Corinthians 15:12). But 'I believe in the resurrection of the body' is part of the historic creed of the church, and cannot be spiritualized away without diluting the gospel.

The good foundation

It is not clear if the foundation of the road is meant in verse 19, or whether this is a new picture. The solid foundation of the church, *the church of the living God, the pillar and foundation of the truth* (1 Timothy 3:15; Ephesians 2:20–22), has been laid by God himself. On this foundation stone Paul imagines two inscriptions, both based on Old Testament teaching.

'The Lord will show who belongs to him' (Numbers 16:5) reminds us that only God knows which of us are his wheat and which are weeds planted by the enemy: knowing God and being known by God is basic (Matthew 7:23).

'Turn from evil and do good' (Psalm 34:14). The first inscription speaks of God's work in calling us, and the second of the need for us to show we are called by a changed life and a firm, continued renouncing of the devil and all his wicked works. Obedience and a holy life demonstrate our allegiance to the Lord. A committed, consistent, beautiful, unselfish life is the acid test of being a born-again person. Note it is not only forsaking vice, but actively performing virtue.

Questions

1. As an imperfect and sinful person how can I be a worker who is 'not ashamed'? Do I have to be a perfectionist? What standard do I have to aim at? Who judges me? Myself? Others? God?
2. In your group discuss ways in which we need to 'cut straight' in our interpretation of the Bible. What wrong approaches should we avoid?
3. Why does falsehood seem to spread so quickly? How have our modern media helped or hindered this problem?

The word of truth

It is clear that the worker who is approved by God will be able to explain clearly 'the word of truth'. But what exactly is the word of truth? Is it the gospel as delivered by Paul to the young churches or is it the fuller and wider truth of the whole of Scripture? Paul does not tell us in this instance, but the answer must surely be 'both'.

A Christian leader ('worker here') must know the Scriptures before he or she can explain them to others. This ought to be obvious but is a principle not always followed. As a first step to understanding how to interpret Scripture try *The Bible with pleasure* by Stephen Motyer (Crossway, 1996) or *How to read the Bible for all its worth* by Gorden Fee and Douglas Stuart (Scripture Union, 1994).

2 Timothy 2:20-26

Sensitive Christianity 2: Sensitive to sin and to people

Paul uses two more illustrations: we need to be useful to God, as a pan is useful to the cook, and gentle and peacemaking just as Jesus was.

The fifth illustration (see p. 187) concerns the various utensils found in a house, some priceless treasures and others cheap disposables: both for banquets and for garbage but both necessary for the running of the house.

At first sight verse 20 seems straightforward: in the church we all have different functions, some people are useful for some things, some for others. But then the train of thought and the application switch in a puzzling way. What does verse 21 mean? To start with there appeared to be a role for all of us – like the different organs of the body (1 Corinthians 12:21–24). Now it seems some pots are to be scrapped and thrown out: is it that we are to throw out of our individual houses all that is shoddy and impure; or that in the local church the weeds are to be separated from the wheat and thrown out? Do you see the problem? It appears that Paul switches from a church application (verse 20) to an individual application (verse 21). How do we solve this?

Servants sensitive to sin

Paul may be speaking of Hymenaeus and Philetus as broken utensils to be thrown out. In Romans 9:21 Paul speaks of pottery for noble purposes and some for common use, and even of 'vessels fit for destruction'. So the cleansing of verse 21 may mean the household of the church getting rid of the bad influence of false teachers. Both the previous verse, *must turn away from wickedness*, and the following verse, *Flee the evil desires of youth*, suggest moral cleansing. Contaminated teaching, and the bad deeds that arise from it are to be 'rinsed out'. Healthy teaching produces healthy lives: sick teaching produces ailing, sinful lives. The illustration is a vivid one.

Are there influences and uncleannesses in our lives which defile us and prevent our being useful? In the old Rwanda revival Christians were thought of as each holding a water pot: the Lord wants to fill them with the water of life, but cannot or will not do so if they are defiled by sin, anger, self-pity, or impurity. Timothy must cleanse himself and his hearers. Then they will be holy, useful and ready for use – clean instruments, sterilized from all sin, whom the Lord can use.

It is easier to urge people to live pure lives than actually to help them to do it. I treasure the memory of a heartcry for relevance from an American student after a Bible exposition of 'Flee youthful lusts' (AV). 'Dr Stott, will you please tell us – how?' The passage itself does offer some solutions.

1. Develop an alternative obsession. The picture is of fleeing from vice (like Joseph fleeing from Potiphar's wife: Genesis 39:12; see notes on 1 Timothy 6:11) and sprinting off in the opposite direction, vigorously running after virtue. This will leave us no time for pursuing vices which will be left far behind. Impurity leads to guilt, lack of assurance and lack of confidence.

2. Invoke the help of the Lord: *Call on the Lord*. Christians are described as those who 'call on' Jesus' name (Acts 9:14, 21; 1 Corinthians 1:2). More is implied than praying, for it means that we believers have the privilege of invoking Jesus' name, as

Roman citizens like Paul could invoke the Emperor and appeal to Caesar. Troubled by 'youthful lusts' we invoke the Lord's name, calling on him to help us. Lord, help me and give me your purity in this situation.

Servants sensitive to people

Paul's final illustration is the Servant of the Lord (see Isaiah 43) and Jesus as the model of the Christian teacher, gentle, peace-loving and conciliatory.

The idea of pursuing *peace* (verse 22) is hard for some of us to take on board. Some of us need to restrain ourselves from taking up the cudgels on all and every occasion: a quiet smile may suffice. 'Pursuing . . . peace' means avoiding needless disputes. The issues raised in 1 Timothy persist (1 Timothy 1:4; 2:8; 4:7; 6:20).

'The Lord's servant' seems to refer to Isaiah 42:1–4 and especially verse 2, 'He will not shout or cry out, or raise his voice in the streets. A bruised reed he will not break, and a smouldering wick he will not snuff out', quoted by the Lord Jesus himself (Matthew 12:19–20). Thus he *must not quarrel; instead he must be kind to everyone, able to teach, not resentful.* More is needed than vigorous hard work and readiness to endure suffering: the Christian worker needs a real sensitivity to people. Being humble and gentle, avoiding pressuring people, is essential in pastoral ministry and in missionary evangelism in hostile religious cultures abroad and at home. We are not just to repudiate those who teach error, which is quite easy, but *gently* to work for their recovery (verse 25) which is much more difficult. False teaching is seen to be the work of the devil (verse 26): a snare set to catch the unwary. It is a horrible thought that as spies can be 'turned' to become 'double agents', so some who seem to belong to God's people might turn out to be working for the Enemy. Hopefully, however, they can 'escape from the devil's trap' (1 Timothy 3:7; 6:9) and be turned back again. It is right to be anxious about divisions in the church, but wrong to react so strongly that the divisions are made worse. This passage is a helpful corrective when our congregations may be divided because of confused and conflicting teachings.

The words to Timothy in this chapter are a challenge to us to be Christian workers today. Our lives can be moulded by these pictures. Are we willing to be:

▶ his soldiers, sacrificing in order to do battle for his cause

▶ his athletes, training and disciplining ourselves for service

▶ his farmers, sweating hard to reap a harvest in his field

▶ his road makers, cutting straight roads, interpreting Scripture

▶ his utensils, cleansed to do his work in the world

▶ his servants, gently instructing others in his church?

Here then are six pictures, six models for us to imitate, and to work at individually for the health of the body of the church as a whole.

Questions

1. Take some time to ask yourself whether you are 'clean' enough to be used by God. What needs to be emptied or scoured out? Talk to God about it.
2. Analyse the second group of three illustrations (road makers, utensils and servants) and apply them to your own lives.
3. How should the 'Lord's servant' deal with argumentative people, the awkward, those guilty of doctrinal error? How does unwise handling of those who disagree lead to divisions in churches, which might have been avoided by gentler dealing?

THE POWER OF
THE SCRIPTURES

2 Timothy 3

A cry from the heart!

An introduction to 2 Timothy 3:1 – 4:8

Paul cries out to Timothy to distance himself from the false teachers described earlier in 3:1–9; 3:13 and 4:3–4. Three times we meet the same identical phrase, a pair of two-letter Greek words, variously translated in English versions as 'You, however', 'As for you', 'But you' (3:10; 3:14 and 4:5). The false teachers are described first and then, by contrast, 'But you'. Timothy must be seen to be different from such people.

There is a second group with whom Timothy must be contrasted. The ageing apostle, chained in prison, is hurting because of Christians who have failed or defected. Phygelus and Hermogenes have deserted (1:15); Hymenaeus and Philetus have swerved from the truth (2:17); Demas has deserted Paul, having loved this world (4:10). Paul has expressed his longing (2:25, 26) that certain unnamed people might be granted repentance, come to their senses and escape from the devil's trap.

In our churches too, we know people who have drifted away. There are weak Christians who settle for the lowest common denominator, so that church standards keep falling. When they cannot even manage that they defect. Those of us closest to them feel sick with the pain and hurt of it: 'Who is led into sin, and I do not inwardly burn', laments Paul (2 Corinthians 11:29). So it is against this tragic background of error and of backsliding that Paul urges Timothy to stay faithful and true. Others may desert and disappear, 'But you ... But you be different'. There is something poignant and touching in this longing for a successor who will continue the good work. But the challenge is to us also: are we significantly different from unchurched people around us: can we pick out Christians from the crowd?

2 Timothy 3:1–9

Outwardly godly but powerless

The vices listed here look like a description of pagan society, but these people are within the visible church.

Paul describes here the behaviour of people in the 'last days'. *There will be terrible times in the last days.* This is familiar teaching about 'the end' so Timothy need not be surprised. 'There will be a time of distress' says Daniel 12:1 and Jesus confirms it (Matthew 24:10, 12; Mark 13:3–23 *etc.*).

Reflecting on the evils of contemporary society, the list of vices zeros in upon the false teachers. *Lovers of themselves* is paired with *lovers of money*, a characteristic of false teachers in Ephesus (1 Timothy 6:10); *boastful, proud* (found together in Romans 1:20) were also used of false teachers (1 Timothy 1:7; 6:4); *abusive* echoes 1 Timothy 6:4; *disobedient to parents*, not providing for them (1 Timothy 5:8); followed appropriately by *ungrateful* and *unholy*. *Without love* (verse 3) implies lacking normal human affection; *unforgiving* is unable to be reconciled; *slanderous* (1 Timothy 2:11; Titus 2:5); *without self-control, brutal* and *not lovers of good* (the opposite of what elders should exemplify, Titus 1:8).

So they lack love and fail to love good, though they love themselves and money: it is a nauseating picture of disgusting people. *Treacherous* (verse 4) means stopping at nothing to gain their ends, *rash* and *conceited* (1 Timothy 3:6; 6:4). The list finishes as it began, asking about the true motives of what people really love and live for: *lovers of pleasure rather than lovers of God*. Sin and inconsistency among Christians can disenchant and disillusion us about the church. Yet Scripture does warn us of this sad possibility.

Imitation Christians

How can people be outwardly pious and inwardly the exact opposite? Such people learn to mimic all that Christians do: it is not hard to imitate external behaviour. Though they look 'religious', they lack true spiritual power. Timothy is to have nothing to do with such people! These are not hypothetical people: they are real people weakening the church in Ephesus at that time. We, today, still face the problem of nominal Christians.

Verse 6 throws further light on the ban on women teaching (1 Timothy 2:12) and the young widows (1 Timothy 5:13). It confirms that some women had been deceived by false teachers. The people described in verses 2–5 creep in under false pretences and gain control over, or take captive 'little women', a scornful diminutive suggesting they are 'easy prey': burdened with a sinful past (loaded down with sins) and, therefore, more vulnerable, the more so in Ephesus with its orgiastic cults. They are *swayed by all kinds of evil desires*, which hints at sexual motives. Their sensuality, perhaps at first unconscious, later develops into something more open. Sects and sex often go together.

These folk feign spiritual interest, *always learning,* as a cover for what has been hinted at in the previous verse. Pharaoh's magicians (verse 8) used magic to copy Moses's early miracles and so hardened Pharaoh's heart (Exodus 7:11–12; 7:22; 8:7). Paul says false teachers, too are bogus opposers of truth. They are people (not 'men') *of depraved minds, who, as far as the faith is concerned*, are rejected. This is the opposite to the 'approved' of the unashamed workman (2:15). *But they will not get very far* or make much progress: compare Timothy's progress (1 Timothy 4:15) and the progress of the ungodly (2 Timothy 2:16).

Revival came to nominal Christians in China, people who had drifted into the church without any true conversion experience, when John Sung and others preached against specific sins: today, we too need to examine our own hearts and lives to ensure we have the power as well as the form of godliness.

Questions

1. In verses 1–4 'lovers of' appears four times. Demas loved the world (4:10). Look at each one carefully and apply them to yourself. What do you really love most? Ask God to show you your hidden motives.
2. What should the churches do about the prevalence of the vices within it, described in verses 2–5?
3. What are the marks of a sect, as distinct from a true church?

A catalogue of vices

This catalogue of vices contains eighteen items: five occur only here in the New Testament; two others are found only in the Pastorals; three are found only here and in Romans 1; four are found only here and in Luke–Acts; leaving four more common expressions.

Where the words appear

	Here only	Pastorals only	Also in Romans 1	Also in Luke–Acts
Number of occurrences	5	2	3	4
lovers of self	Yes			
lovers of money		1 Timothy 6		Luke 16:14

	Here only	Pastorals only	Also in Romans 1	Also in Luke–Acts
boastful			1:30	
proud (x 4)			1:30	Luke 1:51
abusive (x 4)			1:30	Acts 6:11
disobedient (x 5)			1:30	
ungrateful				Luke 6:35
unholy		1 Timothy 1:9		
unloving			1:31	
unforgiving			1:31	
slanderous (x 37)				
uncontrolled	Yes			
brutal	Yes			
not love good	Yes			
treacherous				Luke 6:16; Acts 7:52
rash				
conceited		1 Timothy 3:6; 6:4		Acts 19:36
love pleasure	Yes			

2 Timothy 3:10–13

The first 'But you' contrast: following Paul's example

Paul the apostle is a model of commitment and godly living for Timothy (and us) to follow.

As a young man Timothy was in Lystra when Paul and Barnabas arrived on the first church-planting visit. He had seen Paul stoned and left for dead. He had met Paul again when he returned to Lystra after evangelizing Derbe. The apostles had strengthened the young converts and appointed elders in Lystra, Iconium and Antioch. The third time Paul came, with Silas, he and the elders had laid hands on Timothy and called him as their assistant. Most of us also have learned from the pattern set us by older Christians. We have admired their lives and they have influenced ours. We 'saw' the lives of older believers, who imparted a visual image of how Christians are meant to live, despite the fact that older Christians have feet of clay and feel we are poor, inconsistent human models.

Nine pointers from Paul's life

The word translated as *know all about* (NIV) is a special discipleship word used by Greek philosophers to describe the imitating of teachers by disciples, meaning 'study carefully with a view to reproducing'. Paul then lists what Timothy must imitate, in sharp contrast to the list of vices to be avoided (verses 2–5).

1. *My teaching*, that is, the 'things you heard of me' (2:2). The teaching we hear from others blesses us and makes us want to teach in turn. Good teachers always excite others to start imitating their ministry.

2. *My way of life* means training, upbringing, manner of lifestyle.

3. *Purpose* refers both to God's 'purpose' (1:9) and human 'objectives' (Acts 27:13 AV). Barnabas encouraged new converts in Antioch 'to remain faithful to the Lord with heartfelt purpose' (Acts 11:23, RSV). In the previous chapter we saw that soldiers, athletes and farmers have a strong sense of purpose. Committed Christian leaders impress us, as Paul did Timothy, by their driving passionate purpose to serve the Lord. When Paul was stoned and left for dead at Lystra he did not take early home-leave, but continued on to Derbe next day and then came back to Lystra! Are you also filled with this great life purpose? It is something we disciples all need.

4. *Faith* probably means reliability, faithfulness, fidelity to his Lord. We all need this quality to be faithful followers.

5. *Patience* means forbearance with difficult and irritating

people, and we can usually find one or two in most churches.

6. *Love* for the Lord and fellow human beings contrasts with lovers of themselves, money and pleasures.

7. *Endurance* means the patient endurance of trying circumstances, not the resignation of the bus queue, but the perseverance of the marathon. (2 Corinthians 6:4 provides a parallel list of apostolic virtues, which begins with 'endurance'.)

8. *Persecutions*: being stoned at Lystra was probably the most severe persecution Paul met anywhere short of the final death penalty in Rome.

9. *Sufferings*: Timothy was no starry-eyed idealist for he had seen how Paul suffered in Galatia. With such a model before him, Timothy will not give up when things get difficult. This was the authentic apostolic experience. *Yet the Lord rescued me from all of them* is a triumphant testimony from the more distant past to which Paul will add fresh experience from the more recent past as well as assurance for the threatening future (2 Timothy 4:17–18: Paul uses the Bible to support and strengthen him in his sufferings, here echoing Psalm 34:19, a psalm in which 'saved' and 'delivered' recur again and again). The Lord is not rescuing him from being attacked, or having to suffer, but, so far, from death, its possible result.

Persecution is inevitable for committed Christians (verse 12): in Nepal, Western Christians feel embarrassed that they have never been to prison for their faith!

The first Great Motivation for us as Christian disciples is Christ's life. Secondly, the lives of those who have gone ahead of us, whose examples have shaped our lives and our image of what a Christian ought to be like. *But . . . you* do not be satisfied with anything less than following the best examples: do not settle for being a mediocre disciple. The quality of any group depends upon the quality of its leaders, and the examples they set for new members to follow. According to Peter, Christian leadership is not 'lording it' over followers, but 'being examples to the flock' (1 Peter 5:3). The missionary is responsible for setting a pattern which will inspire others. Christian leaders must cast their mantle over others as Elijah did to Elisha (1 Kings 19:19), so that more Timothys will offer for missionary service.

Paul contrasts persecuted saints with *evil men and impostors* (verse 13), the hypocritical false teachers of Ephesus. Earlier we met the idea of 'Timothy's progress' (1 Timothy 4:15) contrasting with the rake's progress (2 Timothy 2:16; 3:9) and sadly, here it is again. Either we progress from one degree of glory to another, or we *will go from bad to worse, deceiving and being deceived.*

Questions

1. Pray through verses 11–12, asking that you will be able to imitate Paul in the situation you are in.
2. How much persecution do you and your church suffer? Is it 'suffering for the sake of the gospel' because of failures and mistakes, or insensitivity on the part of Christians?
3. Organizations often have a 'mission statement'. Share your personal 'mission statement' and discuss one for your church.

2 Timothy 3:14–17

The second 'But you' contrast: the value of Scripture

We can see living examples of Christian leaders, and read and hear God's living word, the Scriptures.

Timothy, long before he learned from Paul, had learned from two godly women, his grandmother Lois and his mother Eunice. Acts 16:1 tells us that his mother was a

Christian Jewess, but that his father was a Greek. Timothy may have had some identity problems because of his mixed parentage, but he seems to have had a godly home. Make sure you give this to your children, even if you never enjoyed it yourself. Your dreams of a Christian home will not be fulfilled if you are foolish enough to marry an uncommitted partner. Timothy's Jewish mother and grandmother would have begun to teach Timothy the Scriptures from his fifth year onwards, as all Jewish parents did in obedience to Deuteronomy 11:18–21. 'Teach these words of mine to your children, talking about them when you sit at home and when you walk along the road, when you lie down and when you get up'. *'They are able to make you wise'*, says Paul, alluding to Psalm 19:7: 'The statutes of the Lord are trustworthy, making wise the simple'.

Reading Scripture is not a magic charm to save you: salvation comes by faith directed to him who saves (through faith in Christ Jesus). It is not a magic mantra to ward off evil, but a revelation of the will of God which we must exercise our wills to obey. You do not evangelize by telling people to believe Scripture, but to believe in Jesus of whom Scripture speaks.

The Scriptures are inspired

Paul goes on to say two important things about the Scriptures in verse 16:

▶ Their *source* – inspired by God himself

▶ Their *purpose* – they are useful to us.

They are not inspired Jewish guesses about what God might be like, not what people imagine about God, but what God has said about himself and breathed into the Scriptures. It does not say that the men were inspired, but that what they wrote was inspired. The Bible is not merely what spiritual people have thought about God, but what God thinks about mankind. No reference is made here to the human authors, though the thought is similar to that in 2 Peter 1:21, 'men spoke from God as they were carried along by the Holy Spirit'.

The ideas, language, idioms, experience and individual peculiarities of prophets and apostles were not superseded. Nonetheless, God breathed his words into the minds and mouths of men: truth about himself was breathed out by him. When God breathed into the body of man, man became a living being (Genesis 2:7). When God breathed into the words of men they became living words, the Word of God. This is not some abstract and not very useful theological theory. They come from the Lord our Creator. The Scriptures are useful and of great practical importance.

The Scriptures are useful

Verses 10–11 list attributes of Paul that made him useful. Verses 16–17 list attributes of the Scriptures that make them useful. The fact that the first word in both lists is 'teaching' suggests we are intended to see this parallel. We may learn from gifted teachers, themselves taught from Scripture, or directly from the Scriptures themselves. Sometimes we are privileged to hear great Bible teachers, though that cannot be guaranteed in every church fellowship. But that is no reason to absent ourselves from any local church: the Bible is always there to instruct us.

There are two pairs of words: first, in relation to *belief. Teaching* is positive and constructive, while *rebuking* is negative and destructive of false teaching. We not only need to teach truth, but also to refute error. The second pair deal with *behaviour*: here *correcting* precedes *training in righteousness.* Scripture is profitable both for belief and for behaviour: for creed and conduct. Scripture will put your ideas right and your daily living right. *So that* expresses purpose or result in order that *the man of God may be thoroughly equipped for every good work* (verse 17). The expression translated as *man of God* is used in the Old Testament of Moses, David and Elijah, and in 1 Timothy 6:11 of Timothy. In the Greek it actually has the more general meaning, 'person of God' so that 'women of God' such as Miriam, Deborah, Hannah and Huldah (if you don't know who she was read 2 Kings 22:14) may be included. It may mean spiritual leaders in particular, though it must have a more general application to all Christians. You will never be a Christian worker or a missionary leader unless you are taught by Scripture itself.

There is a play on words here because the Greek word translated *equipped* is a compound derived from the same root as 'thoroughly'. We might translate the word play as 'to be complete and completely equipped for every good work'. This is what Ezra, an Old Testament scribe studying in Babylon (Ezra 7:10) did so that he was prepared for the unique opportunity to read the Law to the Israelites assembled before the Water Gate in Jerusalem (Nehemiah 8). It is what Paul did, first studying under Gamaliel and then for three years in Arabia. Paul is always urging Timothy to study hard (1 Timothy 4:11–16; 2 Timothy 2:15) and it is implied here also. If you are going to teach the Scriptures to others in the future, you must first study the Scriptures for yourself now so that you may be equipped for every good work!

Questions

1. Is Scripture the only way to become fully equipped? How does it equip us?
2. How can verses 15–17 help us to develop our own group?
3. How can we help children (our own, our friends' and fellow-believers') to value Bible reading in a television and computer-dominated society?

PAUL'S LAST WORDS

2 Timothy 4

2 Timothy 4:1–4

A solemn charge

Against the threat of the abandonment of truth, Paul urges Timothy to faithful, biblical witness.

Paul has been discussing the usefulness of Scripture and follows with a solemn charge to Timothy to use those Scriptures in his preaching and teaching ministry, in spite of  the interference of false teachers. The charge is based upon the presence of God and the expectation of the return of Christ Jesus as judge.

It seems appropriate as we come to the final chapter, the last of eighty-seven that form Paul's major contribution to the New Testament writings, that this charge to use the Scriptures is delivered in most solemn terms, emphasizing two great truths.

Firstly, *In the presence of God.* We grasp the secret of holiness when we first appreciate that there are no secret sins hidden from the sight of God. In Genesis 17:1 the Lord says to Abram, 'Walk before me and be perfect'. There is no tight spot where Timothy (or we ourselves) are not in God's presence. God is not like some genie in a bottle who has to be summoned to appear: he is always present with us as he promised (see Psalm 139:8–10).

Secondly, *Christ Jesus, who will judge the living and the dead.*

Timothy is reminded that one day we shall all have to give account of how we have used our lives in the service of Christ. These two great truths should govern and motivate our lives. Theology is only theory if you fail to apply it! *His appearing and his Kingdom* reminds us of his coming return in glory. This is not some dispensational theory, but down-to-earth practical Bible teaching: Jesus will come and reign!

The charge contains five commands.

1. *Preach the Word.* That is, be a herald of the royal good news.

2. *Be prepared* is probably a military term meaning to stand by, be ready, be on hand, suggesting the expectation of a sudden arrival or appearance. China Inland Missionaries were told they must 'be prepared to pray, preach, eat or die at a moment's notice': a true apostolic succession. *In season and out of season* translates two words meaning 'good opportunity, no opportunity'. Does this mean convenient or inconvenient for Timothy or for his hearers? We should grab every opportunity we can to teach the truth and preach the gospel.

3. *Correct* echoes the uses of Scriptures (3:16). It means admonish or advise.

4. *Rebuke* or 'warn', as the Old Testament prophets did, and especially of what Jesus did in rebuking demonic forces.

5. *Encourage* as we saw in 1 Timothy 4:13 is not a mere cheering up, but much more specifically expounding Scripture to encourage. And all these five are to be carried out 'with great patience and careful instruction'. This reminds us again of the unashamed roadmaker of chapter 2.

The third description of false teaching is given in verses 3 and 4, again contrasted with the behaviour expected of Timothy: the third 'but you' (verse 5: see next chapter).

For the time will come when men will not put up with sound doctrine (verse 3). The connecting word *For* explains the reason for Paul's charge to Timothy: there will be a turning away from truth and sound teaching. *Instead, to suit their own desires, they will gather around them a great number of teachers to say what their itching ears want to hear.* The prophetic voice is lost when the hearers decide what their teachers must say. The pulpit must not be controlled by the pay cheque. Paul gives a prophetic warning of what he sees coming. It is not unlike some superficial anti-doctrinal trends we meet today. *They will turn their ears away from the truth and turn aside to myths.* We have seen already that Ephesus was a hotbed of mystical speculation (1 Timothy 1:4; 4:7). Gullible people still swallow New Age myths with the same enthusiasm.

Questions

1. How far are you fulfilling each of the five 'charges' to Timothy?
2. How correct is it to welcome the Lord to our services? Is he joining us? Or are we joining the God who is everywhere? What difference does your answer make to the way you approach and experience worship?
3. In what ways do verses 3 and 4 describe the situation we find ourselves in today? Can we still apply the remedies of verses 1 and 2? With what reservations, if any?

2 Timothy 4:5–8

The third 'But you' contrast: fight the good fight

Paul's example of going on to the end of the road.

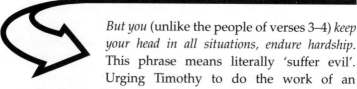

But you (unlike the people of verses 3–4) *keep your head in all situations, endure hardship.* This phrase means literally 'suffer evil'. Urging Timothy to do the work of an evangelist leads Paul naturally into speaking of his own ministry, which is almost at an end. The language of these verses is deeply moving. The emphatic *I* with which the sentence begins (verse 6) has the effect of saying 'as for you . . . as for me' and the explanatory *For* explains why Timothy is given this solemn charge: Paul is about to make his final departure outside the walls of Rome, and wants to hand over to his successor. Paul also uses the illustration of his life as a drink offering (verse 6) in Philippians 2:17, referring to Old Testament 'libations' or drink offerings (Numbers 15:5, 7, 10). Pagans poured out blood, but the Jews used wine instead (Numbers 28:7). Paul's present suffering is like a pouring out of his life blood as an offering to God.

The time has come for my departure. This second picture, also used in Philippians 1:23, is a common way of speaking of death: either as the striking of a tent as soldiers prepare to move off; or

211

the loosing of a ship from its moorings, taking up anchor we might say. Paul feels his death is imminent. The phrase 'Fight the good fight' is often mistaken for a military metaphor, but it is better to translate it, 'I have wrestled a good match' or 'contended a noble contest'. It is followed by another athletic metaphor, 'I have finished the race'. Addressing the Ephesian elders years earlier Paul had said: 'I consider my life worth nothing to me, if only I may finish the race and complete the task the Lord Jesus has given me' (Acts 20:24). Then it was still in the future: now he has finished and his work is done. *Kept the faith* means to be loyal to one's trust. What a challenge to us.

Now there is in store for me the crown of righteousness. Paul refers here to the laurel wreath given to the winner of the Games. The *righteous Judge awarding the crown of righteousness* seems a deliberate repetition contrasting with the Roman judge he will be meeting in court who is not a just judge. Paul knows that he has been justified by grace since his conversion, but at the final judgment *that day* – his assurance will be shown to be securely based. He is not a mischievous dissident, attacking Judaism and undermining Roman government, but a truly righteous man who tells the truth.

Not only to me leads us back to Timothy himself, and indeed *to all who have longed for his appearing.* In Paul's earlier letters he usually uses the word 'Royal Visit' for Christ's Second Coming in Glory, but he also used the word 'appearing' for Christ's 'revelation' six times, all but once in the Pastorals (2 Thessalonians 2:8; 1 Timothy 6:14; Titus 2:13; 2 Timothy 1:10; 4:1, 8). Do we also long for the Day when we shall stop walking by faith and start walking by sight as he finally shows himself to us all?

Questions

1. How significant is human example in showing Timothy the ministry in which he must be involved (cf. 3:10, 11)? What

people have been models for us in the Bible, in history, in our own life?

2. What place does Christ's future 'appearing' have in our daily living? It meant a lot to Paul (verses 1 and 8). What do you think will happen to you 'on that day'?

3. Try writing your own epitaph as Paul does here. If your group has the confidence share the results with each other.

Paul's use of a secretary to write his letters

What do we learn from the following extracts?

'I, Tertius, who wrote down this letter, greet you' (Romans 16:22).

'I, Paul, write this greeting in my own hand' (1 Corinthians 16:21).

'See what large letters I use as I write to you with my own hand' (Galatians 6:11).

'I, Paul, write this greeting in my own hand' (Colossians 4:18).

'I, Paul, write this greeting in my own hand, which is the distinguishing mark in all my letters. This is how I write' (2 Thessalonians 3:17).

'Only Luke is with me' (2 Timothy 4:11).

It seems that Paul had some kind of eye defect (Galatians 4:15), and it is one of the reasons he used a secretary, an amanuensis like Tertius, to write his letters. This may explain the way he includes another name with his own in some letters: Sosthenes (1 Corinthians 1:1); Timothy (2 Corinthians 1:1; Philippians 1:1; Colossians 1:1); Silas and Timothy (1 and 2 Thessalonians). He then seems to have added closing words in his own hand, for which he apologizes. If Luke only was with him, when he wrote his last letter, and perhaps those of Titus and 1 Timothy as well, this (and his use of opponents' slogans) would help to explain why the vocabulary varies between one letter and another. These differences in style have caused many to claim that Paul could not have written all the letters under his name. The fact that he probably used a secretary may help to solve this problem. It is not clear whether we have word for word dictation; or whether the amanuenses took down notes in some early form of shorthand first and then wrote up a fair copy; or even whether it was a kind of composite effort. (Similar issues arise in 1 Peter 5:12 over 'the help of Silas': how far is the polished Greek Peter's or his?)

2 Timothy 4:9–13

Some personal messages

Our friends cannot always be utterly relied on.

Paul needs people

We sometimes imagine Paul as a dauntless superhero clad in emotional asbestos. This passage shows how human he is – revealing his need of human companionship and friendship, as well as normal material and physical needs like warmth and things to occupy his mind. *Do your best to come to me quickly.* In 1:4 Paul said he longs to see Timothy and now urges him to come *quickly* to Rome, and later expresses an even more pressing request *before winter* (verse 21). Paul is alone apart from Luke. Whether Timothy got there before Paul was executed we do not know.

When Paul says that *Demas, because he loved this world, has deserted me,* he uses the same Greek (NIV forsaken) word from

Psalm 22:1 that Jesus used on the Cross, 'My God, why have you deserted me?' *Crescens has gone to Galatia.* Paul is still concerned about the churches planted on the first missionary journey, as well as new church planting in unreached places *and Titus to Dalmatia.* Having been called to join Paul in Nicopolis (Titus 3:12) it would have been natural for Titus to have continued up the west coast of the Adriatic. Paul had spoken of preaching the gospel as far as Illyricum (Romans 15:19), but it seems that the apostolic band is continuing to move northwards along the coast of what we now call Albania and former Yugoslavia. It sounds as if Titus has been with Paul in Rome, so he may have gone from Crete via Italy by ship to Dalmatia. *Only Luke is with me.* Because of Paul's poor eyesight, he needed someone to write his letters, so Luke must have been his secretary for this, and possibly all the Pastoral letters. (See *Paul's use of a secretary* on p. 213).

Get Mark (verse 11). This comes as a surprise. It is a real turn-around in Paul's attitude after his quarrel with Barnabas over Mark deserting them in Pamphylia (Acts 15:38). Paul now describes Mark as *useful* (a word used only three times in the New Testament, here; 2:21 'useful utensils'; and a word play in Philemon 11 on Onesimus's name meaning 'Profitable'). So two useless people, both runaways who deserted their jobs, have become 'useful' through the operation of God's grace in their lives. Paul was great enough to change his mind in his estimation of a fellow Christian. Are there any people we have written off? Should we change our minds about them and give them a fresh chance to serve?

'For I am sending (not *sent* as translated in the NIV) Tychichus to Ephesus'. The NIV once again omits the connecting word 'for', which explains that Mark is needed because Tychichus is leaving, probably bearing this letter to Timothy. Tychichus was also the courier who carried the letters to the Ephesians and Colossians (Ephesians 6:21; Colossians 4:7), though whether on this or some earlier occasion it is not clear. It seems that Tychichus is being sent to Ephesus to replace Timothy, just as either 'Artemas or Tychichus' are going to replace Titus in Crete.

The names Tychichus, Syntyche (Philippians 4:2) and Eutychus (Acts 20:9) were derived from Tyche, goddess of Fortune or Luck, which shows that the early church also had to wrestle with a religiously pluralistic society (note also names like Apollos, Phoebe and Dionysus). Notice that even though he is in prison, Paul is still 'running the mission', arranging his colleagues' movements.

Paul needs things

The old man not only longs for human company, but also for his physical comfort – if winter was coming, he would need his warm winter clothes. Airline baggage limits are restricting enough, but when you had to carry all your luggage with you, walking thirty miles a day along Roman roads, it is not surprising that Paul sometimes left things behind to lighten his load. This verse demonstrates that some Bible verses can only be applied in immediate and local fashion. None of us is stupid enough to *obey Scripture* by making pilgrimages to Troas to fetch cloaks! (See discussion on 1 Timothy 2:12.) Possibly Paul has been rearrested in Troas or Miletus on his way to Ephesus. This passage gives us fascinating insights as we take the opportunity of opening the baggage of a man who 'lived out of a suitcase': he would have carried the tools of his trade: needles and an awl for making tents, proof of Roman citizenship and we now find, *my scrolls, especially parchments*. The first word represents scrolls of Old Testament books, while the second would refer to papyrus notes for sermons, copies of his own letters in codex or book form, some of it now in our New Testament.

Paul needs human company, bodily warmth and things to read, study and write. It is possible that Luke, having collected material for his gospel and Acts, became also the first compiler of Paul's letters.

Questions

1. 'Demas ... loved this present world'. What do you think that actually means? What are the aspects of 'this world' today which turn us away from following Christ?
2. Paul had a team of fellow-workers. How can each of us support and strengthen our own pastor/minister/vicar?
3. Paul 'sent' Crescens, Titus and Tychichus to various places (at great cost to himself). He therefore authorized their ministry. In what ways should missionaries be 'authorized' and 'sent' today?

2 Timothy 4:14–18

Paul leans on the Lord

Although, or perhaps because, Paul's situation is so desperate he is thrown back not on his own resources but on God.

Paul describes just how perilous is his position at this point in his pilgrimage. The details here are so vivid and immediate that it is hard to see how they could be anything but genuine. A writer years after the event could hardly have invented such personal details or such pathos. He saves to the end of the letter what Timothy must have longed to hear first.

A man who did Paul harm

Alexander the metalworker did me a great deal of harm (verse 14). We have heard of silversmiths at Ephesus, now here is a coppersmith, probably also living in Asia Minor rather than in Rome. Alexander may have caused Paul's rearrest by informing the authorities against him. It seems probable that this was the same Alexander, who, with Hymenaeus, was put out of the church by Paul as a false teacher (1 Timothy 1:20: see p. 43).

The Lord will repay him for what he has done sounds vengeful, but perhaps Paul, praying over this man, finds comfort in Psalm 28:4. When we experience 'coppersmiths' in our own lives there is a moral and emotional struggle to forgive. If this man caused Paul's ministry to come to an end, the feeling is understandable. *You too should be on your guard against him, because he strongly opposed our message.* This seems to confirm that this is Alexander of Ephesus. He is still a problem to Timothy in Ephesus, and this explains why he may have been responsible for Paul's re-arrest in Asia Minor, rather than his being a problem to Paul in Rome.

People who did nothing to help Paul

At my first defence no-one came to my support, but everyone deserted me (verse 16). Paul had had a similar preliminary hearing in Caesarea (Acts 24:1–27) before governor Felix, and two years passed before Paul had his second hearing before governor Festus (Acts 25:4). This previous legal delay explains why Paul thought there might be time for Timothy to reach him before his death. It is not surprising that if the case against Paul looked serious, few people wanted to be seen associating with him, especially if Nero was about to persecute the church, as tradition suggests. Psalm 69:20 expresses this sense of desertion. *May it not be held against them* echoes both the words of Jesus (Luke 23:34) and Stephen (Acts 7:60), which Paul must have heard. Both Stephen and Paul are disciples imitating their Master.

The faithful one who did stand by Paul

But the Lord (verse 17) is another striking contrast. In this life-threatening situation, when all human support seems to have been withdrawn, the faithful God is with Paul. The Lord did two things: First, he strengthened (or emboldened) Paul (*cf.* Acts 4:29; 9:28) *so that through me the message might be fully proclaimed and all the Gentiles might hear it*, which seems to mean that Paul was able to proclaim the gospel at his trial. Second, *I was delivered* ('by the Lord' is implied). Is the 'lion' death, the devil, the emperor or what? Nero did some horrible things to Christians, but there is no evidence of the use of lions this early.

It seems fitting that Paul would use the Psalms in times of stress, and we have noted his use of Psalms 28 and 69 already. Probably the language and thought of Psalm 22 lies behind this whole passage, so that 'lion's mouth' comes from Psalm 22:21. Jesus quoted Psalm 22:1 on the Cross, and Paul may have had it in mind (verses 10, 16). The words *I am poured out like water* (Psalm 22:14) may be echoed by *poured out like a drink offering* (verse 6: see p. 211). Other links may be *stood at my side* with Psalm 22:19a and *all Gentiles* with Psalm 22:27b.

Not only does Paul know that the Lord has delivered him in the distant past (3:11) and the immediate past (4:17), but this strengthens his trust that the Lord will continue to rescue him in the future (verse 18). Paul will not necessarily escape death, which seems inevitable. Paul expects to arrive safely in *his heavenly kingdom*. Christians are committed to believe in heaven. What then is more appropriate and typical of Paul than a shout of praise at this point. *To him be glory!*

Questions

1. Can one be a Christian and not believe in heaven? What does heaven mean to you? How can you help others to an understanding of the Kingdom of Heaven and life everlasting?

2. Should Christians always forgive every evil done to them or to others? How can verse 14 help us to arrive at a proper answer? Look at Romans 12:17–21.

3. What assurance does Paul have about God's help in trouble?

2 Timothy 4:19–22

Final greetings

Nine more Christians are mentioned by name in snippets of news and greetings.

Greet Priscilla and Aquila. Paul's old tentmaking friends seem to be back in Ephesus again (Romans 16:3 shows them in Rome). Why, on four out of six occasions,  does Priscilla's name appear first? We know Aquila was a Jew from Pontus, but Acts 18:2 suggests that he met his wife in Italy. Her name may have come from an aristocratic Roman family. Perhaps she was just the more outgoing character and came to mind first.

The household of Onesiphorus, clearly in Ephesus, refers back to the man who sought out and refreshed Paul (1:16, 17).

Erastus stayed in Corinth. Erastus may have been the city treasurer (Romans 16:23) mentioned in the famous inscription discovered near the theatre in Corinth, as the generous donor of pavement; or possibly another Erastus, whom Paul sent on a mission earlier with Timothy (Acts 19:22); perhaps three people, or two or one!

I left Trophimus sick in Miletus. He was the Ephesian Christian who accompanied Paul to Jerusalem, one of those carrying the collection (Acts 20:4). He was the excuse for the riot that got Paul arrested (Acts 21:29). Why tell Timothy in nearby Ephesus about him? Perhaps because Paul left him there just before he himself was rearrested and taken to Rome.

Notice the importance of Paul leaving Trophimus sick. There is no biblical support here for the mistaken notion that Christians ought never to be sick, and would be healed miraculously by an apostle as a matter of course. Christians are not immune either from accidents or bacteria. God may always be pleased to heal, but that is his divine prerogative and we do not have a Christian right to twist his arm to give us healing.

Do your best to get here before winter. Paul repeats his request of verse 9. Once the autumn gales started nobody came by sea: ships were beached and the masts taken down. There is pathos in the old man's longing for human companionship and fellowship in his remaining weeks.

Eubulus, Pudens, Linus, Claudia and all the brothers. Three of these are Latin names, and one is a woman. We know nothing else about them except that they are Roman Christians in touch with Paul (not one of whom is mentioned in Romans 16.) A certain Linus was an early bishop in Rome, a more distinguished bearer of that name than Schulz's character in *Peanuts* cartoons!

Paul's last words

And so we come to the last words of the man used by the Holy Spirit to become the major contributor to the New Testament writings: *The Lord be with your spirit*, addressed to Timothy, and *Grace be with you* (plural), being a greeting to all in Ephesus. Did this letter reach Timothy before Paul was executed? Did he get to Paul before winter? We shall never know. The curtain comes down at this point. Clement, Bishop of Rome (just possibly the Clement mentioned in Philippians 4:3), writing to the Corinthians in about AD 96, wrote a great epitaph about Paul, though he does not give us the details we would like to know!

After that he had been seven times in bonds, had been driven into exile, had been stoned, had preached in the East and in the West, he won the noble renown which was the reward of his faith ... and having reached the farthest bounds of the West; and when he had born his testimony before the rulers, so he departed from the world, and went unto the holy place, having been found a notable pattern of patient endurance.

But the work is not over. After Peter's death, Mark, brought back to Rome by this letter, committed himself to writing Peter's apostolic teaching in his gospel. Luke also would have completed his careful assembling of material (Luke 1:1–4) for his gospel and Acts. The baton of the martyred apostles was passed on successfully to the next generation, and ultimately from them to us.

Questions

1. Look back over 2 Timothy. What has it taught you above all? Can you summarize its message in no more than 50 words?
2. Longterm Christian friendships, like Paul's with Aquila and Priscilla, enrich our lives. Discover what you can about the friends referred to in verses 19–21. What kind of picture does this give you of Paul?
3. Share in your group your problems of leaving someone sick (see verse 20). What priorities may oblige us to leave someone ill, or is caring for the sick paramount? Should we leave our relatives in 'homes'? What are the principles involved here?

For further reading

Commentaries

John R. W. Stott, *The Message of 1 Timothy and Titus* (IVP, 1996).
John R. W. Stott, *The Message of 2 Timothy* (IVP, 1973).
Gordon D. Fee, '1 and 2 Timothy, Titus', in *The New International Commentary on the New Testament* (Hendrikson, 1988).
Donald Guthrie, *The Pastoral Epistles* (Tyndale Commentary, IVP, 1957), especially helpful on authorship.

General

R. T. France, *Women in the Church's Ministry* (Paternoster, 1995).
Lance Pierson, *In the steps of Timothy* (IVP, 1995), a vivid reconstruction of the life and times of Timothy.

Specialist

R. C. and C. C. Kroeger, *'I suffer not a woman' – rethinking 1 Timothy 2:11–15 in the light of ancient evidence* (Baker 1992); a most helpful study of myths in first-century Ephesus and their bearing on the interpretation of this key passage so often misused to marginalize women.
Paul Trebilco, *Jewish communities in Asia Minor* (Cambridge University Press, 1991).
Lelan Edward Wiltshire, 'The TGL computer and further references to *Authentein* in 1 Timothy 2:12' in *New Testament Studies* 34 (1988); technical but helpful for those determined to tease out the meaning of this difficult verse.

Michael Griffiths is minister at large with the International Evangelical Students Fellowship. He taught missions at Regent College in Vancouver from 1990 to 1993 after serving as principal of London Bible College for nine years. His B.A. and M.A. degrees are from Cambridge University.